Engaging Service:
22 Ways to Become a Service Superstar

꧁•꧂

Bryan K. Williams

꧁•꧂

ào•ဆ

B.Williams Enterprise, LLC

ào•ဆ

We exist to serve others so they may better serve the world.®

www.bwenterprise.net

www.engagemenow.com

info@bwenterprise.net

1-240-401-6958

Contents

A Message from the Author
ॐ•ॐ

My passion for writing articles began after a business trip to Chicago. I stayed at one of the city's legendary hotels, and I was thoroughly impressed with the entire staff. One particular bellman was extra special. He served with such poise that I decided to write a thank you letter to him. As I wrote the letter, I realized that others could be inspired to deliver great service as well. Hopefully, anyone who read about this great experience could take away some key points to apply in their respective jobs, teams, and businesses. So I decided to turn the letter into my very first article, "The Greatest Bellman I Ever Met". When that article got published, I received tons of positive feedback from around the world. From that point forward, I decided to write articles regularly.

The purpose for all of my articles is to help readers serve their customers better. This e-book is a compilation of my first 22 articles.

To help on your journey, I have included an activity at the end of each chapter.

1. Complete each activity on your own first, to help internalize the secrets, and to apply ways for *you* to improve.
2. Practice the learned concepts until you feel comfortable with them.
3. Lead your team through a discussion around the chapter, and walk them through the same activity.
4. Share your "aha!" moments; talk through how you are working through some of your own challenges…this level of sharing encourages healthy discussion and communicates that you're all in this together.

My goal for each chapter and accompanying activity is to help you first *gain*, and then *lead* your team to a clear understanding of what a fully engaged customer experience "looks like," and how to "get there," no matter how challenging the scenario.

Make it a great and fun learning experience...on your own and with your team. As always, I extend all my best wishes for continued success!

Bryan K. Williams

❧1❧
I Am a Service Professional

The term "Service Professional" is universal. It is just as applicable to the hotel industry as it is to the healthcare industry and to the taxi industry. Businesses are set up to satisfy a want or a need for current and prospective customers, which means that all organizations are in the service business…whether they care to admit it or not.

It is quite easy for me to tell if a company is truly service oriented. I simply listen and observe how the employees interact with each other. Companies often pull out their mission statements, vision statements, and policies to prove that they are, in fact, service-centric.

> *Being a Service Professional is not about what you do, it is about who you are.*

Those things are important to integrate service into the daily culture, but the true evidence of a service culture comes from what your employees do every day. Are they acknowledging all customers all the time? Are they annoyed when customers ask questions? Do they smile and look for opportunities to anticipate customers' needs?

This chapter is about Service Professionals. If you already consider yourself a Service Professional, then the rest of this chapter will reinforce what you already do. If you're not sure if you are a Service Professional, then use this as a self-assessment. Lastly, if you would like to become a Service Professional, then read on. Being a Service Professional is not about what you do, it is about who you are.

The specific job is almost irrelevant because true Service Professionals will find ways to serve their customers under any circumstance.

Service Professionals…

- Are proud of what they have to offer and it shows
- Make each of their customers feel valued and appreciated
- Ensure that every customer they serve will remember them because of exceptional service
- Personalize their service by giving eye contact (when appropriate) and using the
- customer's preferred name
- Take personal ownership of customer complaints and follow through with the resolution until the customer is completely satisfied
- Take time to research who they will be serving and learn about their preferences
- Always are thinking of ways to not only meet, but exceed their customer's expectations
- Always offer additional assistance

Being a Service Professional is more about a mindset than it is about the specific job. Years ago, I used to shop for music in one particular store. One of the attendants would always let me know about new music being released in the upcoming weeks.

Specifically, one store attendant was a true Service Professional. He embodied the steps I laid out above. In addition to providing excellent service while I was in the store, he would send an email to me with upcoming releases. This went above an`d beyond his job requirements and certainly was more than I expected. Did I ask for the emails? No. Did he allow the parameters of his job to prevent him from engaging the customer? No.

> *Being a Service Professional is more about a mindset than it is about the specific job.*

I was on the phone with an insurance agent not too long ago. In addition to being thorough and very pleasant, she told me that her goal was to earn my loyalty by providing exemplary service. In case you are wondering, this apparently is not a company standard, because no one else says it when I call.

At one point, the phone attendant needed to transfer me to another department to better take care of my specific request. She not only told me she would need to transfer me, but she asked for my permission to be placed on hold, and then waited for an answer. After I replied "yes," she put me on hold, and when she returned less than a minute later, she had the other department on the line, and had already explained to them what I needed. Then, she cordially introduced me to the person whom I would be dealing with.

> *True Service Professionals are your greatest asset. Many companies become successful because of them.*

The whole transfer transaction took less than two minutes, and it won my loyalty. Did she allow the parameters of her job prevent her from engaging the customer? No.

A colleague recently told me about a phenomenal Service Professional she met on a business trip last month. This Service Professional happened to be a taxi driver, and clearly made a memorable impression. My colleague just finished a meeting and caught a taxi to take her back to the airport. On the way to the airport, she realized that her cell phone needed to charge,

> *...he proactively thinks of what his customers may want...even if they don't know it yet.*

and she had forgotten her battery charger at home. For any business traveler, this is a major issue, and when the driver noticed her frustration, he inquired if he may be of assistance. When she asked him to stop at the nearest electronics store so she can purchase a charger, he happily pulled out a neat box that contained a universal battery charger that could be plugged into the car's cigarette adapter. The driver said that his personal mission was to ensure that every customer received a stress free drive so he proactively thinks of what his customers may want…even if they don't know it yet. That was a perfect example of the *Double-Platinum Rule*™ (which you will read about in Chapter 18). Did the driver let the typical expectations of a taxi ride prevent him from engaging the customer? No.

The common theme amongst all three examples is they all contained Service Professionals. They all understood that their ultimate role was to provide memorable service, and the greatest tool was their passion for serving others. The greatest investment you can make to develop a high performing team of Service Professionals is to be very clear on exactly what you expect. Everyone has a different understanding of what it means to provide engaging service…just as everyone has a different understanding of what "clean" is. Be clear. Observe the current Service Professionals on your team and take note of how they engage their customers. Share those examples with the rest of the team. Be sure that the standard is set very high, reward excellence when you see it, and address mediocrity promptly. Service Professionals cringe when they see their manager tolerate mediocrity from co-workers.

True Service Professionals are a company's biggest asset, and many customers will become loyal because of them. They will spend more money because of them, and they will refer their family and friends because of them. Commit to becoming a company that a Service Professional would want to work for in the first place. Let NOW be the time you invest in focusing on attracting, hiring, orienting, training, appraising, and recognizing a legion of Service Professionals to deliver engaging service.

Test Your Service Professional Quotient (SPQ)

1. Using the scale below and the evaluation on the following page, rate your Service Professional Quotient. This is your current level of commitment to deliver a fully engaged customer experience.

1	Strongly disagree
2	Disagree
3	Does not apply
4	Agree
5	Strongly agree

2. Place a check mark in the box under the number that most closely matches your current environment and/or ability to deliver on service.
3. For all questions rated 1 or 2, collaborate with your Supervisor or Mentor to plan actions for improvement.
4. For questions rated "4," create an action plan to get to a "5" rating.

Statement	1	2	3	4	5
I am proud of what my company has to offer and it shows with Each customer interaction.					
I am proud of what I personally offer as a Service Professional And it shows with each customer interaction.					
My team's culture requires and supports doing whatever it takes to make each of my customers feel valued and appreciated.					
I personally make sure each of my customers feels valued And appreciated.					
I make sure every customer I serve will remember me because of the exceptional service I consistently extend.					
I personalize my service by making sure I connect (eye contact, voice connection, etc.) with the customer and use the customer's preferred name.					
My company gives me permission to take personal ownership of customer complaints.					
I take personal ownership of customer complaints.					

Statement	1	2	3	4	5
I follow through with complaint resolution until the customer is completely satisfied.					
My company and supervisor empower me to follow through with complaint resolution until the customer is completely satisfied.					
I take time to research my customer base… who I will be serving …and learn about their preferences.					
I am always thinking of ways to not only meet, but *exceed* customer expectations.					
My company and supervisor empower me to offer additional assistance to customers.					
I always offer additional assistance to customers.					

Action Plan – Improve Your SPQ

All statements rated a **1, 2,** or **4** are now goals for improvement. Use your Day Planner or the provided table (next page) to:

5. List Goals for improvement (first column).
6. Collaborate on steps needed to improve performance. Think outside the box!
7. Set dates with your Supervisor/Mentor for when you expect to see improvement.
8. Set a date to re-evaluate and make sure you have improved your Service Professional Quotient.

As you work toward improvement, think about ways you can see every experience through the eyes of the customer.

Goal	Action	By...
Follow through when resolving complaints	◆ Listen (really listen) to the complaint ◆ List (mentally or on paper) what needs to happen for improvement ◆ Confirm the list with the customer… "What I hear you saying is you need to see A, B, and C to help make this a better experience. Is that correct?" ◆ Work the list ◆ Follow up with the customer and with teammates who you've asked to help deliver (e.g., Accounting Supervisor who can make system changes that you are unauthorized to complete) ◆ Continue until the complaint is resolved **to the customers delight**	5/20/09

Your Personal SPQ Action Plan

Goal	Action	By...

❧2❧
Customer Engagement: Where Do We Begin?

A few years ago, I wrote an article entitled, *The Greatest Bellman I ever Met* (Chapter 14). It was about a bellman that amazed me with his warmth, class, and professionalism. This bellman was not interested in just serving; he was committed to providing an engaging

> *Distinguish between good service, great service, and engaging service.*

service experience. I could literally hear the emotion in his voice when he said "If there is anything further you need while at MY hotel, please let me know". After the article was published in Hotel-Online, I've been asked the same question repeatedly in my keynotes and workshops, "How do we create an army of employees like the bellman in that article?" The short answer is to hire employees who already enjoy serving others, then give

> *Engagement involves a deeper level of service that turns mere visitors into loyal ambassadors.*

them the ongoing support and recognition needed to perform at their best. The longer and more complete answer is to build a culture around customer engagement. Your company's goal should be to create a service experience that fully satisfies every customer.

In fact, you should be interested in not only satisfying your customers; but engaging them as well. Engagement involves a deeper level of service that turns mere visitors into loyal ambassadors.

So let's focus on some specific actions that can be done immediately to jumpstart this culture of engagement. First, the senior leaders in the company must be engaged before they can expect the workforce to be engaged. There's no way to sugarcoat it. Either the senior leaders are fully committed to creating an engaging culture, or they are not. Whatever the

CEO and his/her team deem as top priorities, the rest of the organization will follow. Their commitment must be real and they must have zero tolerance for anything less than success. These leaders must be committed to holding everyone accountable, including themselves, and they must articulate why their vision for exceptional service is more enticing than the company's present reality. Once that foundation is effectively laid, here are some recommendations to assist with your efforts.

Recommendation #1 - Form an action committee that is focused on helping the organization move forward with its engagement efforts. The team should be a cross-section of employees that represent all parts of the organization. This committee should have its own mission statement that keeps everyone focused on their purpose and why their efforts are relevant. They should have the organization's full support and the senior leaders should expect regular progress reports on the team's efforts.

Recommendation #2 - Establish a budget and build awareness on what the organization will be doing and why they are doing it. Constantly communicate the "purpose" of your new engagement initiative, and why it is necessary. Use promotional materials such as banners, posters, intranet, emails, newsletters, and special stationary.

Recommendation #3 - Distinguish between good service, great service, and engaging service. It is important to make such distinctions so that the entire workforce can be clear on what engaging service really means. I've seen many managers declare to their employees, "Starting today, we are going to give better customer service". However, I am confident that each employee that hears such a declaration has a different idea of what "better customer service" really means. For instance, you and I may have different ideas on what a "clean room" looks like. The same is true for service. To align everyone's efforts, there must be clarity around what engaging service looks like, sounds like, and feels like. The best people to explain engaging service are those who are being served. There's nothing more powerful than your customers explaining in vivid detail how to engage them. You can see an example of this on www.engagemenow.com. On the site, you will be able to view a short video called *EngageMe...the voice of your customer.* It depicts engagement from the customer's perspective. Include it in your new employee orientation, show it in your training classes, and view it during town hall meetings. The point here is to build awareness and stimulate dialogue around how the customer expects to be treated.

Recommendation #4 - Take the following seven principles and focus on one principle per week for the next seven weeks. After the initial seven weeks are done, revert back to principle #1 and keep the cycle going. Also consider reviewing each principle during the first week of October, which is National Customer Service Week.

Here are the Seven Principles of EngageMe:

- #1: Create an inclusive atmosphere
- #2: Be eager to serve
- #3: Be welcoming
- #4: Offer a gracious goodbye
- #5: Turn customers into ambassadors
- #6: Create a total experience
- #7: Earn your customers' confidence...reap the rewards

There are worksheets on the following website that can assist with your ongoing discussions on engagement:

http://bwenterprise.net/EngageMe.html

I encourage you to add activities and other creative ideas to keep the topic of customer engagement fresh on everyone's mind.

Developing a service culture is not an overnight process. It requires ongoing efforts to condition the entire workforce into service professionals. The staff must be consistently engaged in order for their customers to be consistently engaged. Creating a culture of engagement begins with you and what you commit to doing right now.

Activity – Put it to Action

1. Over the next 6 weeks, put the following recommendations into action within your organization.
2. Identify key stakeholders and leaders who can champion and ensure follow through on each.
3. Schedule follow-up meetings to discuss current status, elaborate on learned best practices, and answer any questions that arise.
4. The ultimate goal is to have a set plan in place that helps you identify and communicate tangible actions that help create a culture of Customer Engagement in your organization.

Recommendation	Actions
Form an Action Committee focused on helping the organization move forward with engagement efforts	◆ The team should be a cross-section of employees that represent all parts of the organization ◆ This committee should have its own mission statement that keeps everyone focused on their purpose and why their efforts are relevant ◆ They should have the organization's full support and the senior leaders should expect regular progress reports on the team's efforts
Establish a Budget and Build Awareness	◆ Communicate what the organization will be doing and why they are doing it ◆ Constantly communicate the "purpose" of your new engagement initiative, and why it is necessary ◆ Use promotional materials such as banners, posters, intranet, emails, newsletters, and special stationary
As an organization, distinguish between good service, great service, and engaging service	◆ It is important to make such distinctions so that the entire workforce can be clear on what engaging service really means ◆ This will help align everyone's efforts around what engaging service looks like, sounds like, and feels like ◆ Use every opportunity to build awareness and stimulate dialogue around how the customer expects to be treated
Follow the seven principles of EngageMe™	Focus on one principle per week on the following Principles of EngageMe™ ◆ #1: Create an inclusive atmosphere ◆ #2: Be eager to serve ◆ #3: Be welcoming ◆ #4: Offer a gracious goodbye ◆ #5: Turn customers into ◆ #6: Create a total experience ◆ #7: Earn your customers' confidence...reap the rewards
Implement a Plan	◆ Identify a plan for implementing and integrating each principle into your culture ◆ Create key service "cues" that indicate whether each principle is in place within your customer service relationships

೩3ೱ
7 Principles to Fully Engage Your Customers

When I wrote *EngageMe…the voice of your customer* ™ , it was a declaration of how customers would like to be served (Read EngageMe in Chapter 9, page…) . This was regardless if they happened to be in a hospital, hotel, spa, bank, law office, travel agency, or a taxi. The declaration was clear. If you take care of your customers, value their patronage, and provide them with memorable service, then they will return to give you more business. Simple enough. In my quest to help organizations become more service-centric, I've outlined 7 Principles, which are the key learning points from *EngageMe…the voice of your customer* ™. They are:

- Principle 1: Be eager to serve
- Principle 2: Be welcoming
- Principle 3: Create an inclusive atmosphere
- Principle 4: Create a total experience
- Principle 5: Turn customers into ambassadors
- Principle 6: Offer a gracious goodbye
- Principle 7: Earn your customers' confidence…reap the rewards

In the spirit of providing additional insight into these principles, let's review each one.

Principle 1: Be Eager to Serve

Being eager to serve your customer is more about perception than anything else. When the customer walks into your business, is the staff just mulling around or do they appear to be ready to serve? The same applies for service provided over the phone. Does the phone ring 10 times before it gets answered or is there a standard for it to be answered within three rings? This principle is about being prompt in every sense of the word. The customer should not have to wait…ever. If they do, it is your responsibility to apologize for the delay. At the very least, when waiting is inevitable, be sure to acknowledge those customers who are waiting even if it's not their turn. A simple gesture like a smile or eye contact should

This principle is about being prompt in every sense of the word.

suffice. The acknowledgement sends the message that "I see you, and look forward to serving you as soon as possible". Simply put, you and your staff's actions should state, "I am at your service".

Principle 2: Be welcoming

Many companies and service professionals rightfully note that this is the first step of service. No matter what anyone says, true service does not begin without a warm welcome or greeting. I've visited too many places where a blank stare from the waiter, flight attendant or bank teller is supposed to the worthy substitute for a greeting. The purpose of Principle 2 is to let your customers know that not only are you ready to be of service, but that you are happy they chose your business instead of your competitor's. After receiving your welcome, the customers should instantly feel they made the right choice to patronize your business. They should be excited after the initial greeting because you want them to believe that the rest of the service experience will be one hundred times better than the welcome. This is also a great time to get your customer's name so you can better personalize the service experience. Be careful not to overuse the name as it may begin to sound planned rather than genuine. It can just as easily become a customer dissatisfier if used too many times in one service interaction.

Principle 3: Create an inclusive atmosphere

Creating an inclusive atmosphere means involving all parties. In this case, being inclusive is about the service provider creating a relationship that transcends the static nature of a one-way experience in favor of dynamic two-way experience. It is the difference between taking my food order and inquiring about my favorite types of food so the server can suggest the right dishes. It is the difference between selling me a house, and getting to know me and my preferences so you can find the "right" house. It is the difference between the nurse doing basic rounds to check my vitals, and engaging me in light conversation because he/she genuinely cares about my well-being. To be inclusive means to involve the customer in the service they are receiving. The customer is more than just the recipient of the service; they can be an important part of how the service is delivered. Challenge yourself and your team to find out your customers' preferences, then act on them, and share them. It does little good to find out that Mr. Smith likes to be called Mr. S if only one employee knows it. To Mr. Smith, every employee is not only representing the business, but they ARE the business. As such, every employee should not only know what it takes to specifically make Mr. Smith happy, but they should also act on those preferences consistently.

> *Challenge yourself...to find out your customers' preferences, then act on them, and share them.*

Principles 4 through 7 will be covered in Chapter 4. In the meantime, download the complimentary EngageMe worksheets and begin using them with your team. As I travel to various destinations for business and pleasure, I see evidence of businesses that realize the importance of providing great service. They know that competition is always on the prowl to lure away their customers.

I also see many businesses that still don't realize the importance of taking care of their customers and engaging them with exceptional service. These businesses wonder why their sales are sagging and can't seem to attract or keep customers. It is clear that customers expect value when spending their hard-earned money. In fact, the more they spend, the more they expect. So make sure that your service is characterized by being eager to serve, being welcoming and creating an inclusive atmosphere. Service excellence requires effort and with the right mix of dedication, perseverance, and hard work, engaged customers are sure to follow.

Activity – EngageMe™ Role Play

This activity can be done in pairs or as a whole group.

Role-play each of the following principles according to your existing customer service interaction (online, person-to-person, phone service, etc.). Sample scenarios are provided for each.

- **Principle 1: Be eager to serve**

  Scenario: Customer calls or arrives into your establishment and you are on a personal phone call. Work through the scenario as a customer engagement ambassador who is eager to serve. Demonstrate the incorrect way to handle this customer scenario.

- **Principle 2: Be welcoming**

  Scenario A: Customer calls or arrives and is obviously harried. How do you roll out the red carpet and help create a calm and warm welcome for him/her?

  Scenario B: Customer calls or arrives. Warmly welcome them as an ambassador of your business.

  Demonstrate the incorrect way to handle each of these customer scenarios.

- **Principle 3: Create an inclusive atmosphere**

  Scenario A: Customer calls or arrives. Spend a few minutes identifying his/her preferences so you can provide the service that is tailored to meet his/her needs.

  Scenario B: Continue the dialogue from Scenario A and act on those identified preferences.

  Demonstrate the incorrect way to handle these customer scenarios.

Identify one person to play the role of customer, and another person (or group) to play the role of employee. Use these role-play conversations as opportunities to...

- Identify and solve common customer service problems your group encounters
- Exceed the customer service currently given by your group
- Avoid any future issues that may arise

❧4❧
7 Principles to Fully Engage Your Customers – Part 2

There I was…excited to dine in a popular steakhouse with my wife. After all, this night was to celebrate her final day of coursework in her professional degree program. Although we eat out regularly, we especially were looking forward to dining on this night.

The food was good, waiter was good, and service was good…in general, no problems. Afterwards, I told my wife that we won't be going back to that restaurant anytime soon. Why? Because "good" was not my expectation. If I wanted a "good" experience, I would've taken my wife somewhere else with "good" prices. In business, your price point says a lot about the promise you make to your current and future customers. In this case, the high prices (which I don't mind paying) suggests an exceptional, not "good" experience. As a customer, I am expecting the business to create a total service experience…which happens to be Principle #4 from the 7 Principles to Fully Engage Your Customers. If you'll recall, I've already discussed principles 1 – 3 in chapter 3, and this chapter will focus on principles 4 – 7.

As a reminder, here they are:

- Principle 1: Be eager to serve
- Principle 2: Be welcoming
- Principle 3: Create an inclusive atmosphere
- Principle 4: Create a total experience
- Principle 5: Turn customers into ambassadors
- Principle 6: Offer a gracious goodbye
- Principle 7: Earn your customers' confidence…reap the rewards

Principle #4: Create a total experience

Creating a total experience begins with having the right people in the right roles. It means that the greeter must be the person with the most welcoming personality on the team and have the biggest smile. It also means that every person the customer comes in contact with should not only like other people, but they should be happy and excited to be of service. That may sound trivial, but I've been in many businesses where the front line employee's demeanor is sending the message of "leave me alone…I don't want you here". Perhaps the biggest thing to remember about creating the total experience is that the experience is comprised of many touchpoints.

> *Creating a total experience begins with having the right people in the right roles.*

Touchpoints may vary from answering the phone, to escorting a customer down the hallway; the point is that the overall experience is built on individual touchpoints (Touchpoints will be discussed further in chapter 13). At the end of my service experience with your business, if you ask "Overall, how was your stay with us?" I will be responding to the overall experience.

Principle #5: Turn customers into ambassadors

Turning customers into ambassadors is about fostering loyalty. Successful businesses don't measure their success by the amount of new customers they get, they measure success by the amount of business they receive from their existing customers. This is sometimes referred to as organic growth. You want your business to be the first choice when existing and potential customers want to purchase a particular product or service. It doesn't matter if your business is selling rooms, food & beverage, ad space or even hospital beds. Your customers need to know that you look forward to serving them again in the future.

Principle #6: Offer a gracious goodbye

Offering a gracious goodbye is an extremely important principle, yet it can be very easy to bypass. Some service providers feel that after they have given the customer what they paid for, then service is done. Not so. Everything has a beginning and an end. Service is no exception. The purpose of the gracious goodbye is to thank the customer for their patronage. The customer did not have to patronize your business. Every customer should be reassured that their decision to spend their money with you was greatly appreciated. In fact, one best practice is to inquire if there is anything else you can do for your customer. And this is after you have provided the customer with what they came to purchase in the first place; no matter how small the request. After serving my coffee, ask "is there anything else I can do for you?" or some variation of it. The point is that your customers should feel like your job's main purpose is to not just meet, but exceed their expectations.

> *Every customer should be reassured that their decision to spend their money with you was greatly appreciated.*

Principle #7: Earn your customers' confidence...reap the rewards

The rewards here are not just repeat business and referrals. Rewards are knowing that you have made a positive impact on someone's day. You should be confident that the service that you and your team provided made a difference in how that customer views your industry. You are not just doing a job; you are representing your team, your company, and your industry. Like any relationship, earning your customer's confidence is about building trust, and trust is built on doing what you say you will do every time. When I pick up the phone, browse your website, or visit your facilities, I should feel confident that the service will be one of two ways: Just as good as the last time I visited or better than the last time I visited. That is how trust is built.

So commit to fully engaging every customer you have. Feel free to download and use our complementary 7 Principles Worksheets (http://bwenterprise.net/EngageMe.html). Use your team huddles and department meetings to engage your team in a meaningful dialogue about the importance of engagement. As customers become more savvy shoppers, simply competing based on fancy equipment or "bells and whistles" won't suffice. Today's customers want to feel like you value and appreciate their patronage, or they will simply go somewhere else.

Let this be the year where exceptional service is not just a buzzword or flavor of the month. Commit to not settling for "good" or acceptable service delivery from your team (and yourself). Only exceptional service will do. Fully engaging your customers requires dedication, commitment, and action. Follow the 7 principles, and your customers will always follow you.

Activity – EngageMe™ Role Play

This activity can be done in pairs or as a whole group.

Role-play each of the following principles according to your existing customer service interaction (online, person-to-person, phone service, etc.). Sample scenarios are provided for each.

- ### Principle #4: Create a total experience
  Scenario A: Customer calls or arrives. What specific actions do you take to create the total experience for your particular business?

  Scenario B: Customer calls or arrives. Do everything possible to NOT create the total experience for the customer. Ask the group what went wrong and what they would do differently.

- ### Principle #5: Turn customers into ambassadors
  Scenario A: What specific actions do you need to take within your organization to turn a customer with a COMPLAINT into an ambassador?

  Scenario B: What specific actions do you need to take within your organization to turn a NEW customer into an ambassador?

- ### Principle #6: Offer a gracious goodbye
  Scenario A: Offer a gracious goodbye and invite the customer back to visit YOU again.

  Scenario B: Offer a gracious goodbye to a new customer. Determine when they will be back to use your service again.

- ### Principle #7: Earn your customers' confidence…reap the rewards
  Scenario A: Customer calls or arrives with a question to which you do not have the answer. Use your company's vision, mission, and service guarantees to personally earn the customer's confidence.

  Scenario B: You are new to the position and don't have credibility with a long-standing customer, but you're the only one available. However, you know that you're company has empowered you to do whatever it takes to earn the customer's confidence. How will you make sure this customer is confident in YOUR ability to take care of him/her?

❧5❧
Delivering World-Class Service: Function vs. Purpose

What is the difference between the doorman opening the hotel's door and the doorman providing a welcoming experience? Or what is the difference between the housekeeper changing the bed sheets and the housekeeper ensuring that the guest has a clean, comfortable bed to sleep in? Some people may say they are actually the same thing, but others would say that one drives the other. One is the function and the other is the purpose. It is one of the simplest, yet most powerful ways to explain service excellence and how to deliver exceptional service at the same time. Understanding the purpose affects "how" the function is performed. The purpose brings deeper meaning to the function. The person delivering the service is not just robotically serving but understands how he/she is contributing to the company's overall purpose.

The purpose brings deeper meaning to the function.

For those of us who are in the business of taking care of others, this function vs. purpose concept makes a difference on how we are perceived. As a restaurant server, am I just taking menu orders or am I there to help create a world-class dining experience? This may sound simple, but you can easily tell which service workers understand their purpose and those who are merely fulfilling functions. In the service business, our fundamental and primary purpose is to provide a memorable experience for our guests, customers, clients, patients, and residents. This concept is applicable from the taxi driver to the registered nurse and from the travel agent to the receptionist.

On a recent flight, I witnessed a truly great flight attendant, who clearly understood his purpose. He even announced the purpose to the passengers before the flight took off. "Ladies and Gentlemen, I thank you very much for allowing me to serve you today. My purpose on this flight is to ensure your safety and to ensure you are well served." And he said it with a huge smile on his face. He proceeded to explain the details of the plane, a little aviation history, and even commented on the manufacturer of the airplane stairs for goodness sake! He seemed genuinely concerned about passengers not being hit with the beverage cart. After serving the initial round of drinks, he even offered to refill drinks on his way back down the aisle. This man clearly loves his job. I actually told him that I noticed his zest for work. He looked up, smiled, and said, "Well, everyday isn't Christmas!" He also said that being a professional is not about the job, but the attitude one brings to the job. It is performing with excellence regardless of personal circumstances or moods for the day. Surely he was working on a big, luxury plane with ample teammates. Nope, a tiny regional jet...by himself (and the pilots of course).

> *...being a professional is not about the job, but the attitude one brings to the job.*

Contrast that with the gift shop attendant recently at a very upscale hotel. I asked the attendant about the hours of operation for a hotel restaurant, and he told me "I don't know...I just do my time here and go home". He clearly does not understand his purpose.

Those who understand their service purpose believe that going above and beyond is not a chore, but a way of life. So how can companies find these types of people? First, companies don't "create" them, they simply provide a work environment where those types of employees would want to work. Next they go out and hire friendly, professional people. These companies would rather go without the ideal number of staff than having the wrong staff. Why? Star employees don't like working with employees who don't take pride in their work. They get even more peeved when their managers tolerate mediocre performance from the team's under performers.

Regardless of how some staff may moan and give excuses of why they "can't do something", they secretly want to know that you, as the manager, absolutely refuse to compromise. Whether it's cleanliness or taking ownership or greeting every customer, employees are happier and more engaged when they know clearly what is expected of them. They want to work for the best. They want to go home and tell their family

> *...excellence always requires lots of effort.*

and friends how much they enjoy their workplace. Will this require effort on the part of the company? Yes…lot's of it. But excellence always requires lots of effort. Otherwise, every business would be doing it.

As a manager, when you hire someone, should you only talk about the job's function (tasks) or the job's purpose? Is the hostess told that her job is to greet people or to make every guest feel like royalty? Every customer should feel like the hostess has been waiting just for them all day. Are the housekeepers told that their job is to clean rooms, or are they told to make every guest happy by providing a very clean and inviting room?

The point here is to explain the purpose from the very beginning. Then articulate how their specific role is crucial to fulfilling that purpose. Truth be told, even the gardener should know that their primary purpose is to make guests happy.

The specific functions are to plant, seed, mow, etc. If you'd like to take it a step further, each department has a purpose. For the gardener, their landscaping department's purpose is to provide beautiful scenery for the guests. This, of course, supports everyone's collective purpose of making every guest happy. What if you already have a team in place? Then, this is the perfect time to re-orient them with the company's purpose. Some will love it and some won't. The one's who love it will more than likely be your best employees, and the rest will either shape up or ship out (the latter may not be a bad option anyway). But once you make your declaration that excellence is nonnegotiable and every customer will receive the very best, DO NOT compromise.

Help each employee understand not only the purpose of their roles, but the purpose of each function within their role. Then stand back, and watch how even the simplest functions will be performed with more vigor. The trick is to involve each employee in articulating their purpose...don't just give it to them. There can be multiple purposes for one function; and all may be correct.

> *...The trick is to involve each employee in articulating their purpose...don't just give it to them.*

So, the next time you catch your employees performing their functions with a sense of purpose, thank them, and use them as examples for everyone to see. If everyone on your team clearly understands their purpose, the main beneficiaries will be your guest...which is always a great thing.

Activity – Purpose vs. Function

1. Take 15 minutes to define the...

   a. purpose of your job, the "why." It might be helpful to have your job descriptions available for reference.

   b. overall function of what you do.

   c. main functions of your job and the purpose for each.

2. Reflect on and write answers to the following questions:

   - How does my job impact the customer experience?
   - What attitudes do I demonstrate now that could be interpreted as "punching the time clock" vs. purpose focused?
   - What actions can you take right now to change these attitudes?
   - What obstacles are keeping you from getting these?

3. Be prepared to share your findings in a group setting or with your supervisor.

❧6❧
Company Service Standards

When building a strong service culture, it is important to have an inspiring vision and mission statement; but they only provide the context. Company service standards, on the other hand, are the "nuts and bolts" of how you serve. They are the specific behaviors that you expect from yourself and your team in the ongoing journey to deliver engaging service. Standards such as "I attentively listen to others" and "I will always give a gracious goodbye" are clear and apply to everyone from the CEO to the housekeeper.

For service standards to be viewed as credible, they must be discussed frequently. They have to be spoken about everyday and used as the basis for recognition, appraisals, and constructive feedback. Let's assume that one of your standards is "Every team member will maintain an impeccably clean work environment". If one of your

> *These personal service standards are unique to the individual...*

employees walks past a crumpled piece of paper on the floor, that is a great opportunity to discuss that particular service standard. The same applies if a service standard is "I will own and immediately resolve customer complaints, then follow up to ensure customer satisfaction". Talk about that standard when you are recognizing your staff for taking ownership of customer issues and following through. Also, use that standard when providing constructive feedback when the opposite is true. The point is to make the service standards more than just another concoction dreamed up by senior management.

Here are a few easy-to-follow steps when developing or refining service standards:

1. Identify what your customers expect and how they want to be served (Don't assume!). If you don't have a market research department, then conduct your own research by informally surveying your existing customer base. You can start by hosting focus groups. The point is to become crystal clear on what your customers expect from you.

2. Be clear on what type of service your company is promising to deliver. Ensure that your advertisements and other branding messages are consistent with the quality of service you can consistently deliver.

3. Assemble a cross-functional team who will review the collected customer data and begin drafting some preliminary service standards. (Note: be sure to have a senior leader as a member or at least a key sponsor/advocate of this cross-functional team).

   ...the workforce is more likely to embrace anything new or different if they are involved in the developmental process.

4. Get senior leadership input on the preliminary service standards.

5. Revise the preliminary service standards based on senior leadership input (if needed).

6. Share the revised service standards with the company to get more input (remember: the workforce is more likely to embrace anything new or different if they are involved in the developmental process).

7. Revise the service standards again (if needed).

8. Determine how the service standards will be deployed to the workforce (new employee orientation, cards, posters, screen savers, etc.)

9. On a periodic basis, review the service standards for continued relevancy. This is a great exercise during the strategic planning period.

10. In addition to the steps listed above, another great resource to find service standards is the personal service standards already written by your staff.

Use these company service standards to dictate how service is provided on a daily basis. Investing the time and resources to develop, implement, and reinforce service standards will reap enormous rewards in the form of higher morale and more engaged customers.

Activity – Stop, Start, Continue

Use the steps in this chapter to put together a Customer Engagement Plan. Individually or as a group, get started by completing the following questions:

What do our Customers Expect from us?	
What services do we offer to help meet these expectations? (Keep in mind your advertising campaigns, branding messages, etc.)	
What must you STOP doing to deliver on those expectations?	
What must you START doing to deliver on those expectations?	
What should you CONTINUE to deliver on those expectations?	

☙7❧
Engaging Service Part 1: Not Just for the Chic

For those who believe that engaging service only happens in fancy places like chic hotels and restaurants, allow me to share a recent story with you. A few weeks ago, my wife and I were running some errands, and we decided to stop in at a restaurant for lunch. As soon as we entered, there was a huge welcome awaiting us. The hostess, manager, and at least two of the servers all gave a hearty greeting, and made sure we felt like royalty. This was followed by the hostess asking for our permission to be led to our table. Along the way, she explained the history of the restaurant, along with the type of cuisine in which they specialized. She briefly stopped by a glass case that displayed several cuts of meat. The hostess explained that if we were in the mood for exceptional steaks, we could personally select the cut we wished. After a few more steps, she gracefully picked up a fresh basket of steaming rolls for us along the way. At this point, my mouth was wide open by the genuineness, warmth, and attention to detail. To say I was impressed is an understatement. Of course, you must be thinking that this was a super five-star, five-diamond restaurant. On the contrary, it was a casual, barbeque restaurant just minutes away from our house!

> *The hostess explained that if we were in the mood for exceptional steaks, we could personally select the cut we wished.*

The excitement doesn't stop there. The server came to our table within 30 seconds, introduced himself, and welcomed us to "his" station. He told us that he looked forward to serving us and that we should expect nothing less than great service and great food. After returning with our drinks, he gave us a full orientation of the restaurant's ribs and other featured items. I could tell that he enjoyed describing the food as much as we enjoyed hearing about it. Needless to say, the rest of the experience was memorable and the food was unforgettable.

It was obvious that all of the employees in that restaurant clearly understood their role in fulfilling the restaurant's mission of "Legendary Food, Legendary Service". I know what you must be thinking, "Clearly, these were seasoned, professional servers that have spent years honing their craft". Wrong again! Most were young college kids working part-time.

From a leadership perspective, let's take a closer look at how companies are able to create a dynamic environment that promotes fun and quality service all at the same time. Employees become more engaged in their work when they have a clear "line of sight" between their personal contribution and their company's strategic objectives. To bring meaning to their work, your staff wants to know how their individual performance impacts the operation's success. They want to know the expected outcomes or "purpose" of their work. This is completely opposite to force-feeding specific behaviors you want to see performed. There's nothing fulfilling about that.

Delivering exceptional service requires an engaging heart, and such hearts are not motivated by coarse mandates on exactly what to do and say. Instead, of telling the greeters to look up, give eye to eye contact, smile, and say "blah, blah, blah"; explain that their role is to make each guest who enters feel like they are the most important person in the world. Share a story or give an example of the perfect greeting. Ask them to recall a time

> *Delivering exceptional service requires an engaging heart, and such hearts are not motivated by coarse mandates...*

when one of their favorite family members came to visit. Talk to them about how they greeted that family member. Explain that this is how every guest should feel all the time. This is what a service professional is all about.

While they may not say it, they also want to be updated on how well they are performing against your expectations. So schedule regular feedback sessions, post a scoreboard, and share success stories. Ensure employees are getting the information they need to help frame and guide their daily decisions. Above all else, ensure that all employees develop a better understanding of how what they specifically do relates to the company's vision, mission, and goals.

Engaging the hearts and minds of your team is not a passive activity. It requires genuine effort, and that effort will naturally flow into the way service is delivered to all of your guests. So where can you find engaging service? You can find it wherever service is genuine, timely, and warm...for both the team and the guests.

Customer Obsession – Make it Personal

Answer the following questions on your own. Be prepared to share your findings with your Supervisor or in a group setting.

- Is there a "line of sight" between your personal contributions and the organization's strategic objectives?

- What are the expected outcomes (purpose) of the team's work?

- What actions or behaviors must *you* change to create a service-obsessed culture within your group?

Group Share – Brainstorm

Ask a few people from the group to share an experience where the customer service was engaging. Describe the experience, what did a particular person or the organization as a whole do that made you recognize them? Based on this experience, can you describe the vision and mission of that particular company? Now bring it home…

- What about the teams' behaviors or actions must change to become a customer obsessed culture? (Share your own "aha" moments during the discussion time to help your team more openly share theirs).

- What does your team need from you to demonstrate the engaged heart and mind needed to ensure genuine, timely, and warm service?

- How will you celebrate success along the journey? Remember recognition and celebration of service obsession will create the culture you desire?

&8&
Engaging Service Part 2: It's All About the Culture

It's been said that one bad apple can spoil the bunch. Well what if the entire apple tree was bad to begin with? Let's pretend that the "apple tree" is a company's culture, and the "apples" are the workforce. Most times, it is the company's culture that will dictate how the workforce performs. Even if the culture isn't displayed on catchy mottos or mission statements, you can bet that it exists. I've worked with companies long enough to tell what the culture is like by just spending 10-15 minutes observing how the leaders interact with their employees and vice versa. I can also tell by how the staff interacts with their customers. In some cases when there is a poor company culture, there may be a handful of employees who are star performers, and will continue to be stars regardless. More often than not, stars want to be surrounded by other stars and they all take pride in working for a company that has a positive culture. If not, those star employees will either quit and leave or quit and stay. Neither option is favorable. While some readers may file this "culture-talk" away in the land of fluff, please remember that a company's success is a direct result of its workplace culture. That culture will affect everything inside your company, and your customers will see it…good or bad. Allow me to give you an example to illustrate my point.

> *Even if the culture isn't displayed on catchy mottos or mission statements, you can bet that it exists.*

On a recent trip from DC to Miami, I decided to fly with an airline that I normally don't use because of bad past experiences. At any rate, I wasn't surprised that no one, from the ticket agent…to the gate agent…to the flight attendants…to the captain…even to the phone operator didn't smile.

When I went to the gate attendant, she never looked up from her desk. I had to go in front of her face until she eventually acknowledged me. The passenger standing next to me was being given the same type of treatment by another attendant. I then boarded a small bus to be shuttled to the plane. The employee who drove the passengers from the gate terminal to the plane never greeted or gave us a farewell; as a matter of fact, he didn't speak at all. When I boarded the plane, there was no welcome, no farewell, and definitely no smiles. I asked the flight attendant for napkins because of spilled water on my seat, and she told me to "get it from the bathroom". I felt like everyone was just "doing a job". There was no genuine caring, and they certainly did not make me feel like my patronage was valued. Will I fly that airline again? I will try my absolute hardest not to…ever.

I need to point out that by simply reversing what the employees did would not have lead to engaging service. It simply would have been them doing what they were supposed to do in the first place (greet me, be nice during the flight, say goodbye, smile, etc.). Engaging service requires much more.

Could it be that this airline magically hired ALL the apathetic, under-performing employees in their region? Or maybe the pool of applicants is just poor to begin with (which by the way is a popular excuse given by senior managers when their company is known for underperforming). There are, however, other airlines that serve the same markets, hire from the same pool of applicants, and yet give considerably better service than Airline X.

> *There are, however, other airlines that serve the same markets, hire from the same pool of applicants, and yet give considerably better service than Airline X.*

At Airline X, perhaps the outward behavior of the staff is a direct reflection of the workplace culture. It cannot be hidden, no matter how hard you try. Front-line employees don't create the culture, the senior leaders do.

So the obvious starting point is for the senior leaders to become crystal clear on what culture they want the company to have. Then they should engage their best staff throughout the company in determining what it should look like.

Culture-driven leaders are known for bringing out the absolute best from each employee at all times. They believe in their staff, personally role-model excellence, reward superior performance, give timely performance feedback, invest in developing their staff & constantly remind them of what the company is passionate about. They give their vision for the future, and find out the best way to connect the vision to each employee's individual aspirations. Companies that have a strong culture seldom fail…the workforce won't allow it. These managers, supervisors, and employees take too much pride in "their" company.

My challenge to you is commit to being a culture-driven leader. If you want your staff to give 100%, then you must believe in them 100%. If you want star employees, then you must treat your employees like stars. Be known for growing and developing your team, and above all, be known for giving excellent service to your staff and to your customers. Remember, an excellent culture will lead to an excellent workforce that delivers excellent service.

Activity – Culture Driven Leader
S.W.O.T. Analysis

Complete a S.W.O.T. Analysis on your abilities as a Culture-Driven Leader. Answer the questions:

For further insight, continue this analysis with your team. Ask them to complete the analysis on your abilities as a Culture-Driven Leader.

What are my Strengths as a Culture Driven Leader? *(What do I do well?)*

What are my Weaknesses as a Culture Driven Leader? *(What do I need help with?)*

What are my Opportunities as a Culture Driven Leader? *(What are my distinct advantages that I haven't fully used yet?)*

What Threatens my effectiveness as a Culture Driven Leader? *(What cultural, behavioral, or economic threats are holding me back?)*

❧9❧
Engagement – Part 1
To engage the customer, you must engage those directly serving the customer

Over the last few years, one of the main questions I'm constantly asked is, "What is the best way for my company to engage our customers?" My short answer is usually, "engage those who serve the customers". Sounds simple enough…but before you go running to the jewelry store to buy engagement rings for all of your front line employees, let's be clear on what "engage" really means in this context.

For your employees, being engaged transcends just showing up to work and doing what they are supposed to do. It goes beyond constantly being on time and . calling in sick. More than anything, engagement is much more than being "satisfied" at work. Being engaged is synonymous with truly living the culture of the workplace. It is about genuinely enjoying the opportunity to be a part of the organization and noticeably excited about contributing in a significant way…everyday. Engaged employees are your role models; the ones that you'd like to multiply and replicate throughout your company. They are the ones who constantly look for ways to exceed your expectations, and consistently delight customers with their urgency, inclusiveness, and follow through.

Engaged employees are your role models; the ones that you'd like to multiply and replicate throughout your company.

Basically, when you go to work and see that your engaged employee is working, you breathe a sigh of relief, because you know that your day will be significantly more successful.

I'm sure that everyone reading this can point to at least one individual on their team who fits the above description. So the real question here is, "How do you create a team full of engaged employees?" Or at least develop more than what you currently have.

To successfully do that, you must involve your staff in matters that directly and indirectly affect them. Here are six suggestions that you can use immediately:

1. **Involve them in your annual strategic planning meetings.** Even if you don't have an employee actually attend a meeting, make sure that their "voice" is heard. Have a town hall meeting to solicit their input on what the organization should consider as priorities in the future. Hold mini focus-groups with a healthy cross-section of your best line staff. Use data from the employee satisfaction survey. Basically, as you and the other senior leaders gather relevant information to help shape the company's annual strategic plan, be sure to include the voice of your employees. (And make sure they know that you are, in fact, using that data and you value their input).

2. **Solicit their ideas for best practices.** The sharing of best practices is one of the most underutilized practices in many companies. To replicate success you must focus on success. Shine a spotlight on what currently works so that everyone will know exactly what you mean when the term "excellence" is used. By the way, this also encourages your best people to continue churning out more best practices...which is always a great thing.

3. **Get their insight on common pitfalls to avoid.** Believe it or not, your employees, like everyone else, have what's called "tacit" knowledge. Tacit knowledge means knowing something without openly expressing it. For example, Employee A has been working at your company for 7 years, and has seen multiple managers come and go. Chances are that Employee A has knowledge about the company's "real way of doing things" that newer employees don't have...including you and other managers. Employee A has seen when the new hot-shot manager tries to implement new processes...and failed. Employee A has also accumulated a wealth

of insight into what initiatives have not worked, and why they haven't. If you don't believe me, eavesdrop on what some of your tenured line employees are discussing over lunch or in the locker room. You'll be amazed at how much tacit knowledge they really have.

4. So how do you tap into this vast resource? Ask. Many times that's all it takes. Genuinely solicit their insight on what has worked and what hasn't worked in the past. This is especially powerful when it's done during the new manager's assimilation period...usually the first 60-90 days of employment. Trust me, the mere fact that you are seeking their expertise will earn you major points and will simultaneously engage them.

5. **Ensure that each employee's goals are linked to departmental and company goals.** They need to see how their personal performance fits into the bigger picture. You should be able to walk up to any of your employees and ask about the company's mission and get a clear, confident answer. Furthermore, they should also be able to articulate how their department's goals are aligned with the company's goals. If it sounds too good to be true, spend some time with any recent winner of the Malcolm Baldrige National Quality Award (www.baldrige.nist.gov). Employees in those organizations know exactly what makes their company unique, and they also know that their individual contributions are needed and valued.

6. You can begin this alignment process by articulating clearly what the organization's mission is and ensure that all of the employees completely understand it. Then challenge each of them to think of ways they can personally energize that mission. On a monthly basis, all departments should a have a team meeting, and reviewing the department's goals should be a vital part of the agenda. The key here is to link, link, link. Link company goals to department goals, and link department goals to employee goals.

> *Link company goals to department goals, and link department goals to employee goals.*

7. **Show progress on department and company goals**. John Maxwell once wrote that teams can make adjustments when they know where they stand. Just like a stadium has a scoreboard that constantly gets updated, every department should have some easy-to understand tool for tracking key department and company goals. The key points are that the "scores" should be accessible and they need to be easily understood. I have seen many well-intentioned executives take the financial charts and graphs directly from their high-level board meetings and post them on the employee bulletin board. Newsflash: Not everyone has the patience to decipher tables and spreadsheets; especially not a line employee who may not be used to reviewing such reports on a regular basis like a senior manager or executive. Extract the data that is most relevant to that department and show a few key overall metrics that everyone affects.

8. **Foster a culture of effective communication flow and two-way communication.** Make use of every opportunity to connect with your workforce. Utilize town hall meetings, company banquets, cross-functional task forces, and the "Ask the boss" link on the company Intranet. For engagement to take place, employees must feel like the company cares about them as individuals and genuinely wants to see them succeed. You can't fake it…employees know when it's not genuine. Involvement equals more engagement. Solicitation of ideas equals more engagement. Linking personal goals to department and company goals equals more engagement. Regular two-way communication equals more engagement. People like to be involved in the planning of the work that affects them. They crave it; even if they don't verbalize it all the time. So tap into their expertise and they will appreciate you and the organization for it. The end result will be an army of engaged employees whose sole mission is to engage all of your customers all the time.

Activity – Employee Engagement

Using the suggestions discussed in this chapter (outlined below), develop a plan for engaging your employees in your business. Get their input on ways to improve or create a customer-centric culture.

Involve employees in your annual strategic planning meetings.	
Solicit their ideas for best practices	
Get their insight on common pitfalls to avoid	
Ensure each employee's goals are linked to departmental and company goals	
Show progress on department and company goals	
Foster a culture of effective communication flow and two-way communication	

✑10✑
Engagement - Part 2
To Engage...Listen to the Voice of Your Customer

> *Serving customers is an honor that should not be taken lightly.*

Some people believe that poor is the opposite of excellent, while others believe that excellence is the only standard that matters. For those who commit to excellence, providing engaging service is the only standard worth striving for. As a business, providing what you are supposed to provide does not win the loyalty and admiration of your customers. It takes something more. Serving customers is an honor that should not be taken lightly. Being a service professional is a highly esteemed position to be in, and those customers who have been fortunate enough to be served by a true service professional, know exactly what engaging service is all about.

It would be hard for a gentleman to propose to a lady if he did not know who she was; or did not understand the "real" her. What is on her mind? What is important to her? What is she hoping he will provide that no one else can provide quite like him? Knowing the answers to those types of questions will surely heighten the chance of both parties having a successful engagement. This is exactly the case with the relationship between the business and the customer. For the business to engage the customer, it must learn to hear and appreciate the voice of the customer.

What does the customer truly want and yearn for? Chances are that customers choose to patronize your business when they don't really have to. They usually can go somewhere else; like your competitor perhaps.

Therefore, your customers want to feel taken care of and valued. Regardless of the industry, they want to know that they made the right decision when they chose to give you their hard-earned money. Often times, the more they spend, the more they want to feel engaged. And they deserve it.

In fact, if you close your eyes right now, you can literally hear the voice of each customer you serve. They are saying:

Engage me,
Make me feel special,
Make me feel included,
Make me feel valued,
Make me feel appreciated
Engage me,
Tell me that you're happy to see me,
Tell me that you're happy to serve me,
Tell me that you're happy I chose you, instead of your competitors
Engage me,
Welcome me, as if I were a guest in your own home,
Tell me about the service I am about to receive
Engage me,
Thank me for choosing you,
Tell me it was a pleasure to serve me,
Invite me back,
Tell me that you look forward to serving me again…and mean it genuinely
Engage me,
And I will return the favor by being an engaged customer (and your biggest ambassador)
Engage me,
Engage every part of me,
Engage my emotions, my laughter, my curiosity, my anticipation
Engage me,
I want to be your customer…that's why I'm here,
And I will reward you with my patronage, my referrals, and my loyalty,
Engage me.

It doesn't matter what industry you are in, your customers always deserve the absolute best that you have to offer. Just last night, my wife and I decided to visit a Vietnamese/Thai restaurant. It was about 15 minutes from our home in MD so we decided to give it a try. After driving and getting lost a few times, we finally found the restaurant in a strip mall. When we walked in, our expectations were not extremely high, but the staff and overall service experience impressed us nonetheless. The initial greeting was prompt, the server was knowledgeable, and the food runner took great pride in delivering "his" food. It was easy to see that everyone from the manager to the busser was genuinely committed to providing engaging service. To put a memorable conclusion to a wonderful dining experience, the server brought us a tray with two freshly-scented, steaming washcloths. The entire staff then thanked us for choosing their restaurant and wished us a safe trip home. Of course, they invited us back, and needless to say, we WILL go back. They succeeded in turning a potentially bland restaurant visit into a dynamic and engaging service experience.

To recap, everyone on the staff (including the manager) did the following:

- Created an inclusive atmosphere
- Were eager to serve
- Were very welcoming
- Offered a gracious goodbye
- Took pride in turning first-time customers into ambassadors
- Created a total experience that enlivened all of our senses
- Earned our confidence, which will reap the rewards of repeat business (and tons of referrals)

Commit to engaging every customer that chooses your business. Let them know how much you appreciate their patronage and turn them into ambassadors. Starting today, make it a top priority to engage all of your customers, all the time, in all situations.

Activity – Role Reversal

Put yourself in the shoes of your customer, you are the voice of your customer.

- ♦ What is on the customers mind?
- ♦ What is important to the customer?
- ♦ What is the customer hoping your organization will provide that no one else can provide quite like your organization?
- ♦ Pick your favorite line from the EngageMe poem. Why is it your favorite line? And how will you use that line to improve your customer service skills?

With the answers to these questions, this will give a better understanding of what your customers' expectations are. Once we are able to see the other side of our service, we should make adjustments that would satisfy and exceed your customers' needs.

✇11✇
World-Class Service...In a Car Dealership?

When we think of world-class service, images of luxury hotels and country clubs usually fill our minds. What about car dealerships? I know what you must be thinking..."surely he means a Bentley dealership or some other top-line car". Not so...I am referring to a basic car dealership that sells and services medium-priced vehicles, like what you'd find in most neighborhoods. In this case, the car dealership is five minutes from where I live, and they never cease to amaze me with how professional and service-centric they are.

The central theme of this chapter is "any leader in any industry can develop a team of service professionals". That's right...it doesn't matter if it's a grocery store, a mall retail outlet, or in this case, a neighborhood car dealership. To no one's surprise, the dealership's General Manager (GM) is the leader I am referencing here. A few Saturdays ago, I took my car in to get its quarterly service, and since they were pretty full that day, the service associate empowered himself to offer me a rental car for the day while my car was being worked on. I was then escorted over to the sales side of the operation, where I was offered a seat. While waiting for the sales agent to start the paperwork for the complimentary rental, I witnessed something very powerful. The GM summoned for the entire team to gather around for their morning huddle. In this huddle, the GM thanked his team for their ongoing commitment to service excellence and cited

> *Any leader in any industry can develop a team of service professionals.*

specific examples of team members going out of their way to create memorable experiences. He then explained the importance of "connecting" with each customer and making them feel welcomed, appreciated, and cared for. This was followed by asking if everyone had their nametags. After noticing that about four team members did not have it, he promptly asked them to leave and get them (message: your service standards are non-negotiable). He then spent the next five or so minutes conducting role-plays with each team member on providing a warm welcome.

At the end of the huddle (which didn't last more than 10 minutes), everyone was excited to engage each other and the customers. Most importantly, the mantra of service excellence was driven as hard as it could be from the top leader. When I asked one of the team members if the huddle is done every day, she replied, "absolutely". Not surprisingly, this dealership's walls were adorned with numerous awards for service.

From my perspective, here are a few elements that stood out in the service experience, and how much they likely cost the dealership to deliver:

- Using my name = $0.00
- Handshake = $0.00
- Team member giving me their personal phone extension, looking me in the eye and saying "please call me if you need anything else" = $0.00
- Saying "wait here while I bring your car around" = $0.00
- Remembering me and proactively asking about past car issues to verify that they are no longer a hindrance = $0.00

You get the picture; most service standards that create world-class service don't cost a thing. The only price is the senior leader committing to him/herself to hold service excellence as the ultimate reflection of organizational success. In good times and bad...in slow times and busy times...expectations must be clear and accountability has to be solid. If the climate is set by the leader, the workplace engagement and service delivery become much more engaging and fulfilling for all involved.

My challenge to you is to commit to being the service benchmark in your industry. There is absolutely no reason why that cannot be attained. With the right commitment, whatever gets focused on eventually improves. Let this be the year where you focus on selecting service-centric employees, orienting them the right way, let them know what's expected of them, and provide ample feedback along the way (please don't wait until the annual appraisal to do so). Involve those closest to the action in developing/revising your service standards and be sure to reward excellent performance...remember, the best way to replicate excellent performance is to focus on excellent performance.

> *...most service standards that create world-class service don't cost a thing.*

Activity – Cost of World Class Service

Create a list of world-class service standard that are either in place, or would enable you and your organization to deliver engaging service.

Once you have completed your list, calculate the cost of each of these items.

World Class Service Standard	Cost of Standard

1. Place a "+" sign to the left of each standard currently in place in your organization.
2. Place a check mark to the left of each standard you can implement immediately to ensure these standards are in place in your group.
3. Create an action plan to fully integrate these standards into your organization's culture.

❧12❧
Guest Problem Resolution 101: Power of the Follow-Up

A few years ago, I saw some statistics that showed the top reasons why customers stop using companies:

- 9% of customers leave because of competitors
- 14% of customers leave because of dissatisfaction with the product
- 67% of customers leave because of an attitude of indifference on the part of a company employee

I recently had an experience with a telephone company that perfectly reinforced that last statistic. For the past four years, I've consistently used a particular long-distance phone company. Since I had recently moved to a new residence, I attempted to transfer my cable service, utilities, phone, etc. Everything was smoothly transferred except for the phone service. Initially, I was promised the phone service would be transferred on a certain date. It wasn't done. I called back a day after they promised, and they told me it would be done a week later. Still not done. I kept getting transferred from department to department and had to re-explain myself each time. No one from the phone company seemed to take ownership and no one followed up when they said they would. This included the supervisors. I eventually ended my relationship with the phone company and transferred to another phone provider, who connected my service the very next day.

Note: My transfer had nothing to do with the product (phone service). It had everything to do with the attitude of indifference from multiple employees. The biggest issue was that no one followed up with me. If someone had proactively called to give me an update, the relationship may not have ended.

As for the new phone company, the same day I received the service, I also received an automated phone call thanking me for choosing them. I never got around to answering the phone, so they called back the following morning to ask a few questions about all facets of the service experience. Follow up, follow up, follow up.

Follow-up is an art form. Some people have it down to a science. In many ways, one of the biggest differences between good, great, and engaging service is the quality of the follow-up. So what is the first step towards mastering this rare

> *Follow-up is an art form.*

art form? It can be summed up in one phrase: Take ownership. Take ownership of whatever the issue is…that's it. If you receive a complaint or if you are given a request, you own it. It's yours. Don't pretend it's not or hope that the customer complains to someone else. A company I used to work with would say, "You ate it…you own it". Once you own the issue, then the next step is to resolve the issue to the customer's satisfaction. Then, you've got to follow up like you've never followed up before.

Let me give you an example. One of my first jobs in the hotel business was as a towel attendant. Yes, I spent many days in the sun wearing beach shorts, and giving out towels to resort guests. One day, a guest walked up to me, took one look at my name tag and said "Bryan, my suite's air conditioning is not working". Even though I clearly was not dressed like I worked in the maintenance department, the guest asked me anyway. Do you know why?

Because he didn't care which department I worked in. Nor should he have cared. All he should have been concerned with is that I was an employee of the resort; therefore, I should be able to assist. So here's what I did.

- First, I knew I had to own it, then…
- I listened attentively to get the details of the situation (guest's name, room #, etc.), then…
- I apologized to the guest for the inconvenience, then…
- I thanked the guest for bringing the issue to my attention, then…
- I explained what I would do (which was to immediately speak with the maintenance department to fix the issue)
- Then, I re-assured the guest that I would make sure the issue got taken care of.

The purpose of following up is to ensure that the issue has been taken care of to the guest's satisfaction.

Note: Chances are the guest did not think that the towel attendant (me) would personally go up to his room and fix the air conditioning. He did, however, TRUST that the air conditioning would be fixed when he got back to his room.

At that stage, I relayed the issue to the maintenance department…after all, they are the ones who will actually go into the suite and fix the air conditioning. So since I've given the issue to the proper department, my work is done right? Wrong. The maintenance department told me they **would** get to the suite in 45 minutes to fix the problem. So, I then told the guest that the problem will be taken care of in 45 minutes. I'm done now right? Wrong. My next step was to follow up to ensure that the suite, in fact, got fixed. When I checked with the maintenance department, it was fixed! Now surely I'm done right? Wrong. The purpose of following up is to *ensure that the issue has been taken care of to the guest's satisfaction.* So, my next step was to let the guest know that the room had been fixed. This is the platinum rule at its best. Give the guest what they want. In this case, the guest wanted their air conditioning fixed, and it got fixed so now surely all is right with the world. Not so fast.

If the purpose of follow up is to ensure the issue has been taken care of to the guest's satisfaction, how will I know that the guest is satisfied if I don't ask him? So the final step was to call the guest when he finally got back to his room to ensure he was happy with the resolution...which he was. I even sent a hand-written note to the room apologizing once again and thanking him for choosing our resort. Do you think the guest expected for the towel attendant to follow through like that? Absolutely not, but I am sure it left a memorable impression.

The ultimate goal is to follow up until you are confident the guest is happy with the resolution. If you do that, success is sure to follow. While some statistics may show that 67% of customers leave because of an indifferent employee, I would also bet that a significant % of guests are loyal because of a caring employee who takes ownership and follows up.

Leadership Note

To foster this "follow-up" culture within your team, begin with a clear standard relating to owning issues. Relentlessly state that if anyone on your team receives an issue, they own it. It doesn't matter who it is. Then reward positive behavior every chance you get. Do not tolerate it when someone passes along the issue. Keep a follow-up log if you need to. Of course, you must be an example of what you want to see.

Let "ownership" be your key word as you move forward, and commit the rest of this year to foster a culture of follow-up on your team.

Activity – Problem/Resolution

Complete the steps below with 3 or more members your team.

1. Provide each person with an index card. Instruct the group:
   - At the top of your card, write down one guest problem
   - Once complete, pass your card to the person on your left.
   - Once you receive a different card, read through the problem to gain understanding.
   - In the space below the problem, write a new solution on the card (think outside of the box).
   - Trade the card 2-3 times to gain multiple perspectives and solutions to the problem.
   - Once the last person has completed his/her solution, return card to the original "owner"

2. Allow a couple of minutes for each person to read through the solutions
3. Share any new solutions created by the team
4. Use a flip chart to list any ideas that can be added to your team's list of approved actions for solving customer problems

❧13❧
Engage every Customer…One Touchpoint at a Time

Engaging your customers is not rocket science. With all of the available articles, books, blogs, videos and conferences, it can seem that creating an engaging service experience requires a lifetime worth of training. Not true. If you asked me, "how can we improve our service tomorrow?" I would advise you to begin with your touchpoints. I'm sure that you have heard this word before, but I'll go ahead and define it anyway. A touchpoint is any moment of interaction between two parties. If I pass you in the hallway, that's a touchpoint; when you answer the phone, that's a touchpoint; when you open the door for someone, that's a touchpoint. If you think about it, there are literally hundreds of touchpoints in a typical workday. Now here's the interesting part; every touchpoint has either a deposit or a withdrawal. If I'm an employee at Company X, and I pass two customers in the hallway without acknowledging them, that's a withdrawal. If I give eye contact and smile, that's a deposit. Better yet, if I give eye contact, smile, stop, give a greeting, and offer assistance, then that's an even bigger deposit. This same concept works for every touchpoint, every time.

> *Every touchpoint has either a deposit or a withdrawal.*

So how do you identify your touchpoints? The fastest way is to sit in your office and brainstorm by yourself. Unfortunately, you would be missing a tremendous opportunity to involve your staff in matters that directly affect them. If the goal of identifying touchpoints is to engage your customers, then you must first engage those that serve your customers. While you're at it, get your team's input on deposits and withdrawals for each touchpoint as well. Trust me, they will respect you for asking them AND you would have just made a big deposit to your staff! If you haven't guessed by now, deposits equal more engagement and withdrawals equal less engagement.

Back in 2006, I was on board a transatlantic flight from Paris to DC. Since these flights are at least six hours long, airlines tend to offer beverage service at multiple times…especially for those of us who fly coach. When the flight attendants were on their third cycle of beverage service, one passenger asked a flight attendant, "So what drinks do you have?" The attendant looked at the passenger and said, "The same drinks we had 2,000 miles ago!" If there was ever a candidate for the "king of all withdrawals", this was it. The sad part is that I was four rows back and could hear the flight attendant clearly. That means the attendant's statement was a

> *Most passengers will not remember the attendant who made the withdrawal, but they will remember the airline.*

withdrawal for everyone else on the flight that could hear him. The key business point here is that most passengers will not remember the attendant who made the withdrawal, but they will remember the airline. Learning point: All it takes is one employee, one touchpoint, and one withdrawal to lose a customer. On the other hand, one employee, one touchpoint, and one deposit can create an engaged customer.

Just recently, I stayed at a Springhill Suites hotel in Baton Rouge, LA and barely missed the breakfast buffet by a few minutes. As the buffet attendant was cleaning up, she saw the disappointed look on my face when I approached. She told me that she would be happy to get me something from the back. So I asked for cereal with skim milk, and she said that she would return with the cereal right away. The attendant returned with two boxes of cereal, skim milk, and a big smile. She then asked if there was anything more she can do, and when I said no, she wished me a pleasant day. I did not feel like I was an interruption of her job, but the purpose of it. As we examine this touchpoint, there were multiple deposits made:

offered to get breakfast, brought two types of cereal, offered additional assistance, and wished me a pleasant day. The beautiful part is that the entire transaction took less than 5 minutes, and this article will eventually be seen by thousands of readers. Learning point: Multiple deposits encourage free word-of-mouth advertising. In the same touchpoint, multiple withdrawals could have easily been made. The buffet attendant could have pretended not to see me. She could have fled to the back when she saw me coming. Or she could have told me that the buffet was closed, and there was nothing she could do about it. All it takes is one touchpoint.

My challenge to you is commit to identifying your department's touchpoints, and be sure to involve your staff in the process. Then, as a team, brainstorm multiple deposits that can be made for each touchpoint (Hint: There are members on your team already making excellent deposits. Use this as an opportunity to solicit and share them with the entire team).

> *I did not feel like I was an interruption of her job, but the purpose of it.*

Be sure to include a few withdrawals as well. It's amazing how many people make withdrawals and don't even know it.

Let this year be your year for maximizing every touchpoint, for every customer, at every possible moment. Soon you will have a legion of engaged customers who can't wait to tell others about your exceptional service, and how you were able to engage them one touchpoint at a time.

Activity – Depositing Touchpoints

Complete the following chart to identify every touchpoint with internal and external customers. List the deposit(s) that can create customer engagement, and withdrawal(s) that can detract from it. Complete this first on your own, then brainstorm with your group for an even greater benefit.

Touchpoint	Deposit?	Withdrawals?

During group discussion, choose a couple of touchpoints that are most challenging for your group to consistently act upon:

- Identify every touchpoint you have with internal and external customers
- Role play through those touchpoints until your team is comfortable with them
- Debrief:
    - How many deposits were made?
    - How many withdrawals were made?
    - What are some suggestions for turning withdrawals into deposits?
    - What are some ideas for keeping touchpoints fresh and original with your customers?

❧14❧
The Greatest Bellman I Ever Met...

In my current role as a consultant and trainer, I travel quite regularly, and am able to experience service at some of the finest hotels in the world. In fact, I consider myself to be an expert in not only assessing world-class service, but delivering world-class service as well. During a recent business trip to Chicago, Illinois, I stayed at one of the city's finest hotels, and was thoroughly impressed with the flawless execution of virtually every service detail. Particularly, I was privileged to have been "roomed" by the most professional and genuine bellman I have ever met. In strength management, strength is defined as consistent near-perfect performance in a given activity. Basically, that means that someone is doing something so remarkably well, that everyone else looks on in awe as this strength is being displayed (this is easily seen in many professional athletes). This particular bellman definitely has a phenomenal strength for making people feel not only welcomed but treated as royalty. His delivery was effortless, precise, and genuine at the same time.

Allow me to walk you through the service experience as I witnessed it....

After the front desk agent checked me in, she walked around the counter and introduced me to "Tim". He immediately used my name and welcomed me to the hotel, and told me that I should anticipate having a wonderful stay at "his" hotel. As he escorted me to the guest elevator, he gave a thorough description of various hotel amenities such as the dining outlets, spa facilities, and gift shop. He then said that he would meet me at my room in about five minutes with the rest of my luggage that I had given to the doorman earlier.

Sure enough, five minutes later, Tim knocked on the door. When I opened the door, he again used my name and asked if he may enter. Once I said yes, he proceeded in, and immediately asked if the room temperature and lighting was to my satisfaction. Like any five diamond property, he asked me where I'd like my luggage placed. Tim then proceeded to explain all of the room's features including the following:

- Laundry service
- CD player/Radio operation
- Shoe shine service
- Location of In room dining menu
- Location of ice-bucket (which was already filled with ice).

He then asked if I had a laptop with me. When I said yes, he explained the internet connection, and showed me where the internet cable was. He then inquired about laundry, and told me if I had items to be laundered and/or pressed, he would be happy to take them for me. I did, and Tim ensured that I would have them back within two hours (which is what I requested). He then wished me a wonderful stay, and asked if there's anything else he could do to assist.

From a leadership perspective, I am always looking to study success and what type of environment fosters such remarkable excellence to flourish. Usually, there is a clear and unbroken link to leadership. So I asked Tim how long he worked at the property, and he told me 28 years, and loving every day of it. I then asked him what keeps him so motivated to do a great job. Besides the obvious answer of being in the right role and using his talent often, he said that the leadership (especially the hotel's senior leaders) made it a point to consistently solicit his opinion on various service matters, and always made sure that he felt greatly appreciated and taken care of.

This brings me to my next point about how leaders should treat stars. From my travels, one of the biggest misconceptions leaders have is that they should treat everyone on their team the same way. That is probably one of the fastest ways to accelerate mediocrity on a team. Think about it...if I'm consistently doing a superior job, is it fair that I get offered the very same coaching, development, and recognition opportunities as those colleagues who don't put forth the same effort? Don't get me wrong...of course; everyone has to be held accountable for standards of conduct, attendance policy, etc. I'm referring to the amount of effort that is bestowed on various employees. To put it plainly, people should be treated the way they deserve to be treated. In an ideal work environment, people shouldn't even be paid the same. Compensation should somehow be linked to identifiable and quantifiable performance metrics (guest satisfaction, financials, generation of repeat business, etc.).

On sports teams, every athlete doesn't get paid the same. On the Cleveland Cavaliers, LeBron James doesn't get paid what every other player on his team is paid. Why not? He contributes more than everyone else...he scores more, grabs more rebounds, and as a result, more is expected of him, not only from his coaches, but from his teammates and the fans as well.

Now, back to our bellman...he is also the bell captain of this particular hotel. During my visit, I would see him giving feedback to his team (reminding them to smile more, and use the guest's names). It was as though he was a musical conductor in the middle of the lobby, orchestrating (and inspiring) the actions of the team around him.

Clearly, he loved his job, and more importantly, he took exceptional pride in making his guests feel like they have returned home. Whenever he saw me in the lobby, he made it a point to inquire if my stay was indeed wonderful, and if there was anything he could do to assist me. Always very classy, articulate, and genuine. He is a role model of what a world-class service professional should be like.

Tim is, by far, the greatest bellman I have ever met.

Activity – What Does it Mean to Be the Best?

Throughout this chapter, we have discussed actions, behaviors, and attitudes that "Tim" demonstrated as he delivered the best service in the hotel business. What actions and attitudes are required in your business? Complete the graph on the following to help you clearly define what it means to be the best in your business at serving the customer.

Take this activity to your next group meeting. Record answers on a flip chart page as your team brainstorms the possibilities. Note the importance of the overlap between each.

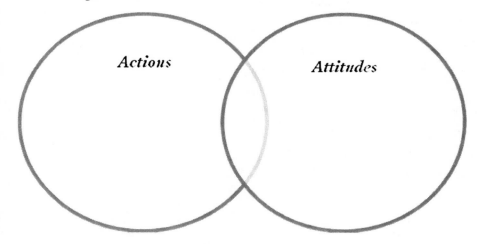

❧15❧
Sorry to say...But Some People Should Not be Serving Other Human Beings

In my travels all over the world, I have been fortunate enough to meet some fantastic people, dine in wonderful restaurants, and stay in world-class (and not so world-class) hotels. No matter where I am or how "acclaimed" the service experience promises to be, one startling revelation hits me over the head time and time again...some people should not be serving other human beings.

On the surface, it may seem like a cynical thing to say, especially coming from someone who makes a living training, coaching, and consulting on the topic of service excellence. The prevailing wisdom from many organizations is that any person can be hired to serve. Given the right tools, training, and coaching opportunities, they too can become a service-delivering superstar. Not so. Being service-minded requires the presence of certain innate talents; namely, "caring", "empathy", "relationship building", and the list goes on. As you've probably observed, some individuals are naturally good at those things, while for others it seems like such talents were surgically removed at birth. That is not to say that in order to be successful, one must be caring or friendly. It just means that "service" may not be their best opportunity to maximize their effectiveness.

From a coaching perspective, what about benchmarking? Conventional wisdom says to put the smile-challenged employee with the service superstar. That seems to work right? If you take employees who do not like to serve people, and tell them exactly how the very best service professionals do it, they still won't like to serve people. It is not about "knowing" what to do, it has to do with genuinely wanting to be of service.

Just last week, for example, I was in a well known electronics store, and I had a basic question about setting up an in-home network. After waiting in line for a few minutes (without being acknowledged), it was my turn, and I thought I would be receiving some assistance. The customer service agent was standing right in front of me but blatantly ignored me…he pretended that I did not exist. After I made a few audible sighs, he finally looked up, although regrettably, and told me that he wasn't ready to help me yet, then walked away. He should not be serving other human beings.

I went to another store. This time, it was a nationally known home improvement store, and I needed some assistance. After hunting for someone who could assist, I finally saw an employee reluctantly assisting a lady. I patiently waited approximately six feet away so I could be close enough to be seen but far enough to not impose. After briefly looking up at me, he continued talking with the lady, then took her to another aisle without ever acknowledging that I may have needed assistance. He might also be a candidate for the "Do not serve other human beings" award.

After some reflection, it is easy to infer that the agent in the electronics store was just having a bad day and that the home improvements store employee was "busy" with the other patron. While both may have been the case, I, the customer, should not have to see, deal with, or tolerate such blatant service tragedies.

So now the important and constructive leadership question to be asked is, "How can my organization prevent such scenarios from occurring?" The first potent answer is to select for service talent. Under all circumstances, do not hire a warm body. Of course, you've heard this before, but selecting for service talent means more than hiring nice people. It means that probing and open-ended questions are asked about what the candidate is passionate about, what they enjoy most at work, and how have they exceeded (not just met) expectations in the past. The ideal responses should revolve around helping, assisting, or serving other people. To paraphrase, one author noted that the best predictor of future performance is frequent past behavior. If the candidates can't give you concrete examples of what they are passionate about and when they have exceeded expectations in the past, then chances are good that service is not a frequent past behavior.

An alternative to selecting for talent is to select for values. As we know, a value is anything that has worth to us. The same way individuals have values, families have values, and of course, organizations have values...whether they are articulated clearly or not. For instance, if one of your organization's top values is responsiveness, then try to select (not "hire") people that at are very responsive.

There are other steps besides selecting the right people, and they will be covered in subsequent articles. For now, here are some points to consider:

- Have a discussion with your staff (individually if possible) and find out what are their true talents. Besides discussions, there are some great assessments to do this. Find out who enjoys serving the customer, who enjoys problem resolution (and yes, there are some people who LOVE problem resolution), who enjoys dealing with numbers, who enjoys organizing projects, etc.
- Give everyone ample opportunity to do what **they** do best with constant support, feedback, and recognition.
- Some people that have been labeled as a "bad apple" may just be in the wrong role. If you don't believe me, try putting someone who loves the back of the house in front of the customer or vice versa...chaos, misery, and frustration may ensue from all parties.
- Above all, to enhance service excellence, you must talk about service excellence, model service excellence and reward service excellence at every given opportunity.

Whether everyone in your organization enjoys serving human beings or not, each person has the ability to make a positive impact if given the right opportunity to shine.

Activity – Steps to Finding Service Talent

Take the quiz below to identify whether you are the right person in the service role? Take this quiz to your group meeting. Once these questions are answered open up a discussion about the answers.

Questions	Yes	No
Do I enjoy serving the customer?		
Do I enjoy problem resolution?		
Do I enjoy dealing with numbers?		
Do I enjoy organizing projects?		
Am I a service superstar?		
Do I receive ample feedback?		
Do I give feedback to my employees?		
Do I receive adequate support		
Do I give support to my employees?		
Do I receive recognition?		
Do I give recognition to my employees?		
Am I in the correct role?		
Are my employees in the correct role?		
Am I rewarded for service excellence?		
Do I reward for service excellence?		

❧16❧
Healthcare: The Highest Form of Hospitality

When we look at the word "hospitality", it is no coincidence that "hospital" encompasses most of it. I firmly believe that healthcare is the highest form of hospitality. This word typically generates images of hotels, restaurants, and spas. Many people in the healthcare industry, however, don't think of themselves as hospitality professionals. Having the honor to impact a person and their family's life in a deeply memorable

> *Having the honor to impact a person and their family's life in a deeply memorable manner is a great position to be in.*

manner is a great position to be in. In the hotel industry, people don't NEED to stay at hotels. Not getting upgraded to a suite or receiving a warm bottle of champagne can hardly be considered life-threatening emergencies. With healthcare, people need you. As such, there is a large social responsibility that goes along with being a healthcare professional. Regardless of what position you may have (nurse, physician, receptionist, housekeeper, department manager), you directly impact the service experience that patients receive.

As a service excellence consultant/trainer, my clients are in disciplines ranging from public school systems to commercial real estate. Many, however, are in healthcare…by far. Without fail, the consistent question that I get is "Does this service excellence stuff really apply to Healthcare"? It doesn't matter if it's a health system, hospital, dentist office, community health center, or senior living community. My answer is always the same…Yes! The universal concepts, tools, and practices of service excellence are not only transferable, but in an ideal scenario, the healthcare industry should be the global trend-setters in the area.

From my work with various organizations, I have found that the most effective ones establish, develop, and sustain a culture of service excellence by focusing on three areas:

- Setting the foundation for service excellence
- Enhancing the patient experience
- Gaining physician involvement

Setting the Foundation

When building a house, one of the first major construction activities is laying the foundation. Great care is taken to build an extremely strong foundation with the right materials, and with the right people doing the work. Only then, can the rest of the house be built. A weak foundation equals a weak house, and a strong foundation equals a strong house. Even if a massive storm blows through, everything else may topple, but the foundation should still remain. It should be sturdy, unshakable, and reliable.

The same is true of an organizational foundation. For service excellence to be considered a priority in the healthcare setting, it must be a key piece of the foundation. The foundation includes elements such as the mission, core values, and operating principles. I have seen many healthcare institutions boast their newly created mission which its executives worked so tirelessly to craft. Even with a supremely articulate mission statement on their walls (with a gold frame no doubt), there may still not be a systematic and sustainable change in service delivery. Why? Most times, the answer lies with what I call the "key". This key unlocks the organizational service potential that lies within. I am referring to the organization's senior leadership team. Of course, the CEO is not out there treating the patients, but believe it or not, that person along with his/her team of senior leaders impact how that patient is treated and what type of service experience all patients receive.

To put it as plain as possible, the priorities of senior leaders become the priorities for the rest of the organization. If providing patients with a memorable service experience is not critically important for the senior leadership team, then it won't be critically important for their direct reports, and subsequently, the organization. Some CEO's mistakenly believe that showing "support" means writing a memo to endorse the service initiative.

> *Drafting a memo does not come close to tirelessly proclaiming that the war cry of world-class service will not go away.*

Drafting a memo does not come close to tirelessly proclaiming that the push for world-class service will not go away. Sending a memo is a nice start, but the real impact is seeing all senior leaders modeling the service behavior they want to see replicated. That means not blindly walking by people in the hallway (patients and staff), and that also means using people's names, and continuously looking for ways to not just meet, but exceed expectations. The service mission has to be talked about…all the time. It can't, under any circumstances, be perceived as just another "flavor of the month".

The staff will soon realize that striving for service excellence is here to stay when they see their senior leaders:

- Consistently reward those who deliver memorable service as defined by the patient.
- Hold non-conformers accountable (management and line staff)
- Make "service excellence" a part of daily informal conversations around the institution. (use regular team huddles if you need to)
- Include the topic of "service excellence" in all meetings (yes, even the financial meetings).
- Regularly spotlight examples of "service excellence" as performed by the staff in places like the company newsletter, Intranet, and bulletin boards.

This all sounds good, but still may not be sufficient. What will truly move the service needle from *good to great*, then from *great to world-class?* The answer may very well be a hearty dose of dissatisfaction.

As I say in all of my classes, "Dissatisfaction fuels Action". When there is enough dissatisfaction with the current state, then action can begin to take place. This is true not only of organizational improvement, but of personal improvement as well. Think about it, whether the dilemma is weight loss, saving money or taking that long-awaited vacation, it is the dissatisfaction with the present that drives action to accomplish something in the future. It doesn't mean that the dissatisfaction is a bad thing. Most world-class healthcare organizations that I am familiar with are so pre-occupied with the grander visions of the organization's future, that they have self-imposed a healthy mixture of current appreciation and dissatisfaction for the status quo. These forward thinking healthcare providers know that patients and workforce talent have a myriad of choices of where they choose to go, so the big differentiator lies not only with which institution has the fanciest equipment, but who is known for taking special care of those within that institution.

Patient Experience

Regardless if the situation is a painful hangnail or a terminal illness, the service experience is ultimately defined by the patient. Interestingly enough, that service experience rarely has much to do with how many credentials a care provider may have or how new the equipment may be. It is the feeling of being genuinely cared for and the staff's ability to anticipate needs that sets the service experience apart from the norm. We all "know" this is important but how can we take it from the realm of superficially interesting (but fundamentally insignificant), to the realm of critically important? It starts with each care provider, from the CEO on down, defining in clear terms, what defines service excellence in their respective roles.

Questions to ask yourself are:

- Who is my primary customer? (could be internal or external)
- What does that customer expect? (how do I know?)
- What are all the various ways I interact with that customer? (these are your touchpoints)
- How can I enhance each of those touchpoints?
- What can I do to make each service touchpoint a memorable one?

Delivering service in a manner that conveys empathy is one of the best ways for the care provider to connect with the patient on an emotional level. Giving updates and briefing the patients on the status of their condition and tests may also contribute to a caring atmosphere. Stating, "I can only imagine how you must feel" and "I'm here for you" can work as well, depending on the situation of course. Proactively taking an interest in the patient's family and learning about their hobbies and other interests can convey empathy. We can write down an entire list of what can be done to show empathy, but the actions won't be genuine unless there is a naturally empathetic care provider doing the empathizing. Otherwise, the potentially memorable service interaction can spiral into a robotic and emotionally placid experience. Ensure that the right people are in the right positions to create memorable experiences.

Physician Involvement

I have heard some healthcare executives say that hospitals don't have patients, physicians do. The assumption is that the hospital's primary customer is the physician, and in order to stay competitive, the physicians must view the hospital (or any other institution) as a worthy place to practice medicine.

We all know that physicians create enormous value for the institution by building lasting bonds with patients. Often times, their alliance to a particular institution is influenced by their personal alignment to the organization's values, and their confidence in its key leaders. In other words, physicians make a personal decision to work with healthcare leaders who make them feel good about practicing medicine at their facility.

A popular quality management principle is to involve stakeholders in the planning of the work that affects them. As a primary stakeholder, involve physicians in matters such as strategic planning and recognition activities. The management team should be encouraged to attend medical staff meetings to ensure alignment and cohesiveness. Building ongoing opportunities for candid communication between physicians and the management team can help bring down the invisible wall that exists in many healthcare institutions.

The same best practices that have made stellar reputations for various hotel and retail companies are just as applicable for those in healthcare. Healthcare organizations like Bronson Methodist Hospital, Robert Wood Johnson University Hospital Hamilton, and Baptist Hospital, Inc. were all winners of the prestigious Malcolm Baldrige National Quality Award (the nation's only presidential award for organizational performance excellence). They are proof that service excellence is not only attainable in healthcare, but can also be performed on a world class level. When it comes to the health of ourselves and our loved ones, we all desire the best service experience possible. It is time for all healthcare organizations to claim their rightful place as leaders and trend-setters in the delivery of world-class service.

Activity – Group Work

Now it is your turn to take these steps into action as a group, take the point of view of the organization as a whole:

- Setting the foundation for service excellence
- Enhancing the customer experience
- Gaining employee and customer involvement

Create a pyramid with the foundation at the bottom and put in buzz words and actions to assist the group to see how these steps can be used on each level.

Gain employee and customer involvement

Enhance the customers' experience

Set the foundation for service excellence

ஐ17ஓ
Where Does Service Excellence Begin?

I work with organizations all over the globe, and there is one question that I am always asked, "Where does service excellence begin?" In other words, they want to boil it down to the very beginning, and fully understand what steps should be taken to successfully embark on this service excellence journey. If I can just bottle up the answer in a magic pill for senior leaders to administer to their staff, I would not have to work another day in my life.

> *The journey really begins with what the senior leaders consistently think, speak, and do.*

Suffice it to say, the "answer" to the service excellence question is not that simple...however, it's not that complicated either. The journey really begins with what the senior leaders consistently think, speak, and do. Then it trickles down to what everyone else in the organization consistently think, speak, and do. The point is this...service excellence is not some abstract milestone that the company will achieve "at some point"; it begins with what you do...right now.

Now, let's take this discussion and focus on three important variables. First, you must be absolutely clear about what is "world-class". Next, you must understand the power behind creating your own reality. Finally, you must fully leverage the power of your organizational values to steer your journey.

What is World-Class?

Let's start with the abstract concept of "world-class". In the Olympics, if an athlete wins the gold medal, that award becomes a tangible symbol that represents the absolute best in the world. However, in many industries, there is not a definitive symbol such as a gold medal to show who the best is. For us who serve others for a living, it can truly be a subjective assessment (by the way, when I say "serve others", I am referring to any organization that has customers, regardless of whether you call them guests, clients, tenants, patients, residents, members, etc.). In my courses, I often ask if someone wins a race, would that person be considered the best. Usually everyone in attendance says yes. Then I ask, "Would that person be considered world-class"? There's often a mixed reaction. My next question is "What, then, truly defines world class?" Is it simply being better than everyone you consider to be your competitors? Or maybe it is your competitors in your geographic region. You might also consider world-class to be the top in your industry…right? Maybe not. Being the best among your competitors, in your region, or even in your industry does not qualify your organization as world-class. Frankly, it is possible to be the best of a bad bunch…so the word "best" is truly relative. A word like "world-class", however, conjures up images of people, teams, and organizations that transcend their industry. The mere image of their name or logo generates a feeling of excellence that is more than just being the best.

As it relates to service, world-class can mean doing basic things in such a consistently excellent manner that it is rare to find that type of consistency elsewhere…in any industry. This reminds of a telephone customer service representative that I dealt with less than two months ago. Now I don't know about you, but my experiences with customer service reps (over the phone) are usually very poor. Not so in this instance. I was fortunate enough to be served by a true service professional by the name of Stacy. She was a telephone service rep for a health insurance company, and I called the company to get some much-needed assistance for a number of things that went wrong with my service. In such situations, I usually get passed around from person to person like a hot potato, but not this time. Stacy stayed with me through the entire conversation. Even when she would have to call another department or company to assist, she never left; in fact, Stacy would always explain the scenario to the new party so that I wouldn't have to re-explain myself each time. I was never cut off and she consistently paraphrased me to ensure that she understood the message I intended to convey. In short, Stacy made me feel heard, served, and cared for. Both Stacy and her company stood out as world-class because the level of attention and follow through was unforgettable, and the service was astronomically better than any other company…in any industry.

Now, how can you develop the Stacy's of your organization who absolutely love to provide world-class service? Well, it is NOT by studying average. If you want to deliver world-class, you must understand world-class, and to understand world-class, you must study world-class. Let world-class organizations be your benchmark.

In my days as a Director of Quality at a luxury hotel in Atlanta, GA, one of my responsibilities was to analyze guest satisfaction data for the property, then compare that data to other hotels. One morning as I was briefing the executive committee of the property, I started with the average performance amongst the other properties, and I was stopped by the General Manager. He asked, why I was reporting on the average. He emphatically stated that the hotel's goal was not to be average, but to be at the top of the list. So from then on, the hotel's sole comparison, were only the top hotels.

Key Takeaway
Give your staff an assignment to research and report on an example of world-class performance, and why they believe it is worthy of being called world-class. Have them tell you what lessons can be learned and immediately applied from such performance?

Define your reality

The second key point in the service excellence journey is to define your reality. In elaborating this point, we will look at three principles from a field of study known as "Appreciative Inquiry". They are the constructionist principle, anticipatory principle, and the enactment principle. The constructionist principle states that "words create worlds". This basically means that the words we use directly lead to the reality we see. Or as Joseph Jaworski once said ..."we don't describe the world we see, we see the world we describe". The concept is that there is a correlation between how you refer to your employees and how you actually perceive them (reality). Try it...say the following terms, and gauge your perception; associate, lady, employee, staff member, team member, member, partner, gentleman, etc. Do the same thing for how you refer to those who patronize your business. I know a major department store that refers to their customers as guests. Can you tell the reality they are trying to create?

> *...the words we use directly lead to the reality we see.*

Next, there is the Anticipatory Principle. It states that we move in the direction of our images of the future. The vivid images of the future directly impact our present-day actions. *Key Point: The stronger the vision, the stronger the action.* When the images of the future is very clear, human systems organize their present actions (consciously and subconsciously) to reach that vision. This is why having an organizational vision is so critically important. World-class companies don't just have the vision statement printed on glossy paper or posted on the company website. The best leaders use that vision to guide, inspire, and remind

> *World-class companies don't just have the vision statement printed on glossy paper or posted on the company website.*

everyone in the organization of the grander future that is in store for everyone.

The third piece is the Enactment Principle. The best way to explain this is by using one of Gandhi's most famous quotes..."Be the change you want to see". I'm sure you've heard this sort of thing before, but if you want your team to greet every person who walks through that front door, guess who must be the biggest greeter of them all? You! If you want every email to have a complete sentence, guess who must lead the charge? You! If your hope is that every customer has their preferences acted upon, guess who must be the first to act on their staff's preferences? You! Once you've finished modeling the desired behavior, ensure that everyone is held accountable for those service standards...including yourself.

The value of organizational values

The final piece of this service excellence puzzle is probably the most overlooked asset in most companies: The organization's core values. The reason that values are so underappreciated is because most executives file them away in the land of "fluff". How much value can the values bring anyway? First of all, if service is not a dominant organizational value, it will not be valued...period. Values, in the truest sense, are basic, enduring, unshakable, fundamental, and absolute. They are meant to be taken literally, and acted upon. There should be an obvious connection between what the company is known for (hopefully service), and the values.

Many times, the organizational value of "customer's come first" never was meant to be taken literally or used as the basis for managerial decision-making. So how do you breathe life into those values? Putting values into action starts with saying what you mean, and meaning what you say-or not saying anything at all. It can actually do more harm than good by having a value like "everyone is empowered to make decisions", then not showing support for those who took the value seriously. In short, if the value is not something you are willing to relentlessly talk about and hold everyone accountable for, then don't put it as a core value. Your staff and your customers will respect the organization for being "true" to itself and not trying to go along with every industry trend. The values are meant to inspire and navigate the organization through good and bad times. They don't just drive the business; they drive the people within the business.

> *If the value is not something you are willing to relentlessly talk about and hold everyone accountable for, then don't put it as a core value.*

As you can see, service excellence truly is an organizational journey that links what is genuinely believed to what ultimately is done on a consistent basis. It doesn't matter where your company or team currently is on this journey. Remember to keep the vision of service excellence clear and inspiring; then let that vision pull the entire organization towards it like a magnet. Developing or transforming an organizational culture doesn't happen overnight, but with the right vision, leadership, confidence, and values, it is very attainable.

So you ask, "where does service excellence" begin? It begins with you.

Activity – Group to Group Exchange

Use the space below to list different ways to promote Service Excellence in your organization. As you review your list, identify ways to personalize excellence at every step in the customer experience.

Take this activity to your next team meeting and:

1. Split the team into 2 groups

2. Each group will need to think of different ways to promote Service Excellence.
   - Allow them to use ideas in the article
   - Encourage the team to expand on these ideas and make them personal
   - Allow each group 15 minutes to complete this task

3. Encourage everyone to ask questions to get clarity on how to personalize and act on these ideas

4. Compare and contrast ideas discussed

❧18❧
The Double-Platinum Rule ™

Whenever I deliver a keynote, training workshop, or explain my company's service philosophy, I begin with an in-depth discussion on the three service rules. They are the Golden Rule, Platinum Rule, and Double Platinum Rule. Surely, you've heard of the Golden Rule, which basically states that you should treat others the way YOU want to be treated. Not everyone has heard of the Platinum Rule, which focuses on treating people the way THEY want to be treated. If you haven't met me, then chances are that you have not heard of the Double Platinum Rule...that's because I conceived it a few months ago. Knowing the way my mind works, there will probably be a Triple-Platinum Rule coming soon also. So before I get into the Double-Platinum Rule and its implications for creating and delivering an exceptional service experience, let's discuss the first two rules.

The Golden Rule

In one of my sessions recently, I asked for the meaning of the Golden Rule, and someone blurted out, "He who has the gold makes the rules!" Not quite the definition that most of us are familiar with. In short, this rule is about treating others the way you want to be treated. If I want to be treated nicely, then I should treat others nicely...if I want to have doors opened for me, then I should open doors for others...and if I want to be greeted with a big hug and high-five wherever I go, then I should give a big hug and high fives to others right?....Not so fast. While the Golden Rule is a good baseline to have when developing the empathy muscle, it only works when other people want to be treated the way you want to be treated. To put it another way...treating people the way you want to be treated only works when other people want to be treated that way. Otherwise, you may end up turning people off.

This can be a difficult pill to swallow for those who pride themselves on knowing exactly what others want…even without asking them. Why wouldn't all guests want to have a personal escort and tour to their room? Why wouldn't everyone want to hear the evening news in a taxicab? Why wouldn't everyone want to be told "Good Morning" and engaged in conversation? The point here is that if you are committed to creating an exceptional service experience for each customer, then each customer's wants, needs, and desires have to be acknowledged, celebrated, and acted upon. Each guest must feel as though they are the only ones in existence when being served. You owe it to them. After all, chances are they had a choice whether to patronize your business or not. Each time a customer, guest, or patient chooses to be served by you, they are basically saying "I've chosen you…now show me why I made the right decision".

> *While the Golden Rule is a good baseline to have when developing the empathy muscle, it only works when other people want to be treated the way you want to be treated.*

This now brings us to the next rule…

The Platinum Rule

If the Golden Rule is all about what you want, then the Platinum Rule is about what your customers want. So the Platinum Rule states "Treat others the way THEY want to be treated". Although it sounds like common sense, it's not as common as you might think. This rule means that you recognize that service is not about what you want to give; it's about what others want to

> *If you give me what I don't want, then you haven't increased your value in my eyes.*

receive. If you give me what I don't want, then you haven't increased your value in my eyes. There must be a deliberate effort to uncover your customer's wants, needs, and desires in order to take the guess work out of the equation. It doesn't matter if you "know what you're talking about". If you haven't captured information to support your hypotheses, then it's considered anecdotal. So my advice is to optimize the various ways your customers can give you information. Use telephone surveys, focus groups, questionnaires, feedback cards, etc. Once you confidently know what your customers want (because they've told you), then you can proceed with meeting and exceeding those expectations. Of course, I thought this all made perfect sense. After all, when it comes to service, what else can be more important than giving customers what they want? The answer hit me upside the head a few months ago…

The Double Platinum Rule ™

I'll explain this rule by giving you the inspiration behind it. A few months ago, I went out to my car only to find that the front right tire was stolen…completely gone! So after storming around upset for a few minutes, I put on the spare wheel, and drove to the nearby auto store. After explaining to the attendant that my wheel was stolen, I proceeded to order a new wheel. The attendant obliged and I was told that the wheel would arrive by the following day. Great! As I was leaving the store, the manager stopped me to ask if I got everything I wanted. After telling him yes, I briefly explained my wheel mishap from that morning. He then asked in a verifying manner, "So you also ordered the wheel locks, right?" Now don't laugh, but up to that point, I had never heard of a wheel lock. The manager told me that it prevents tires from being stolen, and I should consider ordering some. So, I went back to the attendant that I placed the tire order with, and asked why he didn't recommend the wheel locks…especially after I told him that my wheel was stolen. He then looked me in the eyes and said, "I was doing my job and giving you what YOU wanted". Wow, that's the Platinum Rule! The implications immediately hit me. The attendant had given me what I wanted, but I was still upset. As I was driving back home, I thought about the Platinum rule and how it may not be sufficient in all situations. So the Double Platinum rule is (you guessed it), "treat others the way they don't even know they want to be treated". To boil it down…anticipate, anticipate, anticipate. Don't just meet your customer's expectations, EXCEED them.

Grounding your service strategy in the three Universal Service Rules works well, because it heightens your empathy (Golden Rule), encourages a keen focus on your customer's expectations (Platinum Rule), and challenges you to consistently think of ways to exceed those expectations (Double Platinum Rule).

So I encourage you to share the rules with your team and no matter which one is being discussed, you'll know that service excellence is top of mind.

Activity – Discovering the Double Platinum Rule

Create two scenarios that are common within your work environment.

Using the table below, write how service will be different for each "rule".

Don't forget…the Golden Rule may not necessarily take the customer's preferences into consideration…the Platinum Rule discovers and meets the customers' expectations…the Double-Platinum Rule exceeds the customers' expectations by anticipating their needs.

	Scenario #1	Scenario #2
Golden Rule		
Platinum Rule		
Double-Platinum Rule ™		

✑19✑
Service Excellence: A Destination or a Journey?

Appreciate where you are, but imagine where you could be. That is the mantra of continuous improvement. World-class hotels, restaurants, and spas are never content with the status-quo. Good is not good enough. They believe that running an exceptional operation is like studying for a 100% on a test; they will prepare for 100% accuracy, but if they get a few wrong, they may still get an A…which is far better than a C.

Dissatisfaction fuels their action. Don't get me wrong; these organizations are not clinically depressed. It's just that their vision of the future is much grander than the reality of the present…even if the present is not so bad. Some of the most successful companies and CEO's I know are the most aggressive when it comes to

> *Make dissatisfaction your friend, your coach, your advisor.*

improving on what they have already perfected. Dissatisfaction fuels their action. Make dissatisfaction your friend, your coach, your advisor. Most of us have made sustainable changes in our lives

ONCE we've gotten dissatisfied or fed-up enough. Dissatisfaction with the present can provide the necessary fuel to propel us from "should" to "must". There's a big difference between we "should" be a world-class restaurant and we must be a world-class restaurant. In fact, dissatisfaction with a dining experience inspired me to articulate the customer's expectation. The end result is the product line: EngageMe…the voice of your customer.

Regardless of what industry you are in, as long as you have customers, you are in the service business. It doesn't matter if they're called customers, guests, patients, students, tenants, or clients. Service is service, and to become known for providing exceptional service, you must commit to continuous improvement. Even if you're good, you can be great, and if you are great you can be world-class. Truly world-class service companies have become best friends with "continuous improvement". Excellence really isn't a destination; it's more of a journey…a mindset…an attitude towards how the business is run. Like everything else in life, continuous improvement must be conditioned into being. It won't happen automatically.

A big part of transformation is to keep the momentum going. Share your vision with the entire workforce. Make use of every opportunity to bring service excellence to the forefront of everyone's minds. Show videos, display posters, and use worksheets to stimulate team dialogue around service excellence. Talk, talk, and talk some more…be committed. Once service excellence becomes an organizational norm, all you have to do is support, encourage, and recognize excellent performance. Don't make the mistake of spending the majority of your time focusing on weaknesses. While your opportunities for improvement may hinder your success, the fastest and most sustainable way to reproduce excellence is to focus on excellence. Excellence breeds excellence. Success breeds success. Discover what everyone on your team is exceptionally good at, and encourage them to focus on and apply those strengths throughout the day. Try it. You'll see that they will be happier, more productive, and more engaged in their work. For example, if your company has been making positive strides in your customer satisfaction scores, take the time to analyze and study what your team did right. Then standardize and deploy those best practices throughout the workforce. Remember, study success to

> *…study success to understand success, and once you understand success, then you can replicate success.*

understand success, and once you understand success, then you can replicate success.

If you have already begun the process of transforming your culture, congratulations to you! There is a big difference between wanting to do something and actually doing it. I heard a riddle once that really made this point clear for me. If there are two frogs on a lily pad, and one decides to jump off, how many are left on the pad? The obvious answer is one frog…right? Actually, there would still be two frogs left on the pad. You see, one just "decided" to jump off; it wasn't mentioned whether the frog actually jumped or not. When it comes to commitment, how many times have we "decided" to do something, but never actually followed through with doing it? In the context, of the hospitality industry, many companies want to elevate their level of service which usually entails transforming the organizational culture to become service-oriented. Needless to say, that type of cultural transformation does not happen overnight. It requires intense commitment, discipline, and follow-through. A compelling vision combined with decisive action is a potent prescription for sustained success.

So what breakthrough will you have? What is your compelling vision? What are you currently proud of? What can't you tolerate any more? What do you refuse to accept as you move forward?

The clearer you become about why the present is no longer acceptable, then the future becomes irresistible. From the luxury to economy market segments, let continuous improvement become your mantra for sustained service excellence.

Activity – Your Dreams Come True

Analyze your current work environment. Use the space below to complete this activity.

1. List recommendations and strategies you would implement to create the ideal service excellence culture. Think outside the box…no rules or limitations – time and resources are not a problem.

2. Beside each recommendation/strategy, write the different strengths, barriers/limitations, risks, and requirements

3. Based on the limitations you've identified and your current environment, highlight recommendations you can realistically implement right now. Which can you implement in 6 months? In one year?

Take this activity to your next team meeting.

1. Divide the team into groups.

2. Tell them their dreams have come true.

3. Provide instructions above for each group…ask them to brainstorm together to come up with different ideas and strategies

4. Give them 10 minutes to complete the project.

5. Ask the group to list the different strengths, barriers/limitations, risks, and requirements related to these ideas

6. Compare the groups' ideas and limitations to your own list

7. Agree on ideas you can implement and work together to create a realistic timeline.

8. Don't forget the long-term ideas…as your customer service relationships improve, so will your profits and resources!

❧20❦
Service...It's not about what YOU want to give

Webster's Dictionary defines service as "work done for others". Yet, it is interesting to find so many businesses in the hospitality industry doing the exact opposite. Many incorrectly believe that service is about the great product or idea that everyone must want. I mean, why wouldn't a customer want to have an in-depth conversation at 6AM in a taxicab? Why wouldn't the non-Turkish customer want to listen to loud Turkish music during a shuttle ride? Why wouldn't the guest want to have their newspaper ironed? All of the previous questions, although asked in a sarcastic manner, are true events of what some in the hospitality industry deem as "service".

As this article's title states, service is not about what you want to give; it is about what the customer wants. For any service provider to remain relevant in today's marketplace, it is critical to not just react to customer expectations, but to actively solicit them as well. According to the Baldrige National Quality Program's "Criteria for Performance Excellence", it is important for organizations to establish how they gain "knowledge about...current and future customers and markets, with the aim of offering relevant products and services". If the customer doesn't deem it as service, then it is not service. Of course, such a revelation can strike a blow to anyone who prides him/herself on being service minded.

Let's take "Rick" for example. He is a supremely talented gentleman who took great pride in taking care of his guests. His job was a poolside concierge at a luxury Caribbean resort, where he was responsible for engaging the guests around the pool and offer any additional insight and/or up sell the resort's amenities. He once told me, "I can't wait to go to sleep at night so I can wake up in the morning to come to work". Rick loved his job. Being a poolside concierge, he was out in the sun all day which meant that he was constantly sweaty…understandably so. He felt that his service to a guest was not complete unless he gave them a big hug. His intentions were good, but many of the guests, judging by the grimaced looks on their faces, didn't want to be hugged by a happy, sweaty guy. After some coaching, he calibrated his service approach to exclude the sweaty hug…thus ensuring a more satisfying service experience.

Just recently, I called for a taxi to pick me up at 6AM to take me to the airport. Now, anyone who knows me can testify that the hardest part of my day is getting out of bed in the morning. Suffice it to say, I am not really a morning person. So I got into this cab half asleep, and within a few seconds, the cab driver starts peppering me with questions about where I'm from, where I'm going, and if I enjoy traveling. After about five minutes, I politely leaned forward and explained to the cab driver that I'm usually much more responsive, but I really didn't get much sleep the night before. One would think that the driver would get the picture. After about one minute, he starts peppering me with questions again! This continued for a few more minutes, until I finally, and politely, told him that I'd rather not have a conversation since I'm not fully awake. He got the message, and altered his approach to be accommodating rather than forceful.

I understood his frame of thinking; the driver is supposed to make conversation with the customer…after all, that's what he was trained to do. I'm sure that he was also taught that engaging in a conversation would certainly lead to a bigger tip. The intent was good, but the purpose was missing. Service is not about what you want to give…In that moment, during the cab ride, ultimate service would have looked something like this…

- The driver would have greeted me, and taken my luggage to put in the trunk.

- He would have opened my car door and inquired if the temperature was fine, and if I'd prefer to listen to some music (even asking my music preference would not hurt)

- Seeing how early it was, and my obvious state of sleep walking, he could let me know that he sees that I'm sleepy, and offered to stop at a nearby gas station or fast food joint for a coffee. (I happen to not be a coffee drinker, but the offer would have earned him some serious points.)

- Giving me an approximate estimated time of arrival (ETA) to the airport would have added to the experience.

- Upon arriving at the airport, open my door, retrieve my bags, and offer me a business card.

- Finally, thank me for choosing company "x", wish me a safe trip, and offering his company's future services.

If anything remotely close to what I just described actually happened, my tip to the driver may have increased substantially. My emotional engagement would have grown...not only to the company, but to that driver as well. It is also important to note that virtually nothing on the bulleted list should cost the driver any extra money. The rewards in terms of repeat business and word of mouth advertising would have been priceless.

While it is more natural for some people to have deference to the customer, just beginning with the premise of "service is about what the customer wants", will be a great starting point for success.

Activity – Picking up on Cues

This is a group activity to help your team use customer's cues and signals to anticipate and meet their wants and needs

Choose 2 volunteers. One volunteer will display characteristics of a dissatisfied customer, the other volunteer will play the role of customer service superstar.

Coach the "customer" to give silent cues that they are no longer engaged with your business (verbal and body language).

The "superstar" should be able to pick-up on these cues and give the customer exactly what he/she wants.

Scenario - *The customer is asking the superstar about a product or service you offer. The experience has been wrought with mistakes. For example, the customer has seen or talked to four different people before getting to this point, had issues with their credit card when trying to complete the transaction, and their original request has yet to be fulfilled. Regardless of who is responsible for these mistakes, this customer is ready to "win";they want to complete this transaction without any more hiccups.*

Debrief: *Highlight cues a customer may give in your environment. Make the point that superstars of service excellence can pick-up on these cues and give the customer what THEY want.*

☙21☙
Hiring & Engaging a World-Class Team

When I was hired over a decade ago to join a hotel, the general manager told me that if in 6-months the team was not better as a result of me being hired, then I've failed. Wow, what pressure! He explained that, just like on a sports team, the primary purpose of bringing in new players is not to take up space on the roster, but rather to help the team win more games. At that moment, I realized that he was not just looking for another "warm body". I could tell that this would be a different place to work. This would be a place that valued my contributions as a person, and one that let me know that my work ethic and dedication would DIRECTLY influence the success of the team. If you're wondering what the job was…it was as a busboy in the hotel's restaurant.

Surely, such high expectations are usually reserved for managers and senior leaders. Why would the general manager place such high expectations on an employee who cleans tables and brings bread to the table? Simply put, the general manager's vision was to have a world-class team, and world-class teams have world-class employees…in every role. Even if I was mopping the floor, I had to be world-class.

The focus of this article is on the on-boarding experience for new employees. The on-boarding experience includes the recruitment phase, hiring phase, orientation phase, and department training phase. Each phase should reflect your team's commitment to excellence and affirm the important role that the employee will play in achieving the team's goals. The best way to get a team of world-class employees is to set the expectation very high from the onset. So what should be done in each phase?

Recruitment Phase

- Include your company's motto, mission statement, and purpose statement on every advertisement. Include them on your application as well.
- While the application is being filled out:
  - Show a video of what you stand for
  - Show a video of employee testimonials
  - Show a message from the CEO or another senior leader
- From the beginning of the recruitment phase, applicants should feel like this is not *just another job*. This is a special place to work. A place where everyone is expected to be a service professional and perform with excellence every day. They should also feel like they will be treated with excellence by the company.

Hiring Phase

- During the first face-to-face interview, ask "Why do you want to work **here**?" Anything resembling, "I'm looking for a job" should be a red-flag. I suspect that you want employees who believe in your company and yearn to be part of a winning team.
- Ask about the applicant's experience delivering great service. Listen for specific examples…not hypothetical's or what-ifs. Remember, you are looking for people that naturally enjoy service. If they naturally enjoy serving others, then they should have recent examples.
- In addition to the standard Human Resource questions, ask other questions that align with your mission and values. For example, if "taking ownership" is an important team value, ask about specific times when they took ownership of a situation. The point is to hire professionals whose personal values mirror your team's values. If the match is right, you have a recipe for a successful, long-term relationship.
- Your ideal prospects should feel like your team is the place they have been looking for their entire careers or the place where they would like to establish their careers.

- Assemble a panel of your best employees conduct peer-interviews. This is a great way to keep your best staff engaged! If you want great employees, then involve your existing great employees in the hiring process.

Orientation Phase

- Orientation is meant to be a significant, emotional experience.

- This is your opportunity to treat your new employees the way you would like them to treat their customers.

- If the orientation is robotic, procedural, or lacks emotion, then that is how the majority of your team will serve their customers.

- Ensure all signage is clear leading to the orientation room. Everyone should know who the new employees are. Wouldn't it be great if the employees involved in the interview process were at orientation to greet the new employee?

- Ensure every new employee has an attractive name tent and professional handout materials. This is to show that you are prepared for the new employees.

- Select a panel of current employees to give testimonials and to answer questions. This can be a very memorable part of the orientation.

- Senior leaders should be involved to communicate the culture of the company.

Department Training Phase

- The transition from new employee orientation to the department orientation should be seamless.

- A representative/mentor/trainer from the new employee's department should be present at the end of orientation to greet the new employee.

- The new employee can be presented with a packet that includes a welcome letter from the team, work schedule, training schedule, and department specific information.

- Establish a cross-training schedule for your new employees that include time to spend in other primary departments. This will help build empathy and interdependence between departments.

- Bring the employees back at least 1-month later for an orientation reunion. This is to see how the new employees are doing and to solicit their feedback on ways to improve the team.

With an effective on-boarding experience, your new employees will be excited that they've finally found a company that cherishes excellence. Your commitment to hiring the best will also re-engage your existing employees. They will be happy with your commitment to only hire and orient the best applicants. Whether you are hiring a busboy or a general manager set your expectations high and excellence is sure to follow.

Activity – Looking for World Class Employees

This activity is designed to assist managers create a plan to find world class employees.

The steps and suggestions from the article are listed below. Take notes on those not in place in your organization to create a plan for engaging world-class employees. Discuss this activity at your next meeting…gain your team's insight and input on these suggestions.

Recruitment Phase	Notes
What is your current Recruitment process?	
How can you incorporate your company's motto, mission statement, and purpose statement on every advertisement and recruiting materials?	
What can you provide during the application phase to communicate to candidates: • What you stand for • How satisfied your current employees are • Information from your CEO or another senior leader that invites star candidates to join your company	
What is your potential employee's attitude about your company?	
Hiring Phase	**Notes**
Do you currently have a list of questions for prospects?	
Does your list include questions like… • Why do you want to work **here**? • Ask about the applicant's experience delivering great service	
Take a look at the values of your organization; do your interview questions on those values? If not, make sure they do.	
Assemble a panel of your best employees to conduct peer-interviews.	

Orientation Phase	Notes
Is your orientation impactful? Orientation is meant to be a significant, emotional experience that bonds new employees to your "brand".	
Use this as an opportunity to treat your new employees the way you would like them to treat their customers.	
Select a panel of current employees to give testimonials and to answer questions. This can be a very memorable part of the orientation.	
Are your senior leaders involved in orientation? Senior leaders should be involved to communicate the culture of the company.	
Training Phase	**Notes**
What type of training do new employees receive?	
The transition from new employee orientation to the department orientation should be seamless.	
A representative/mentor/trainer from the new employee's department should be present at the end of orientation to greet the new employee.	
Present the new employee with a welcome packet. The packet can include a welcome letter from the team, work schedule, training schedule, and department specific information.	
Establish a cross-training schedule for your new employees that include time to spend in other primary departments. This will help build empathy and interdependence between departments.	
Bring the employees back at least 1-month later for an orientation reunion. This is to see how the new employees are doing and to solicit their feedback on ways to improve the team.	

❧22❧
Making it Stick

Every year, I'm more convinced that the Baldrige framework is the closest thing to a silver bullet when it comes to systematically improving an organization (www.baldrige.nist.gov). Even when a small fraction of the framework is applied, improvements are inevitable.

> *...there has to be just as much (if not more) time spent on the sustaining side of the equation, as on the introduction side.*

This week, I was thinking about the various companies that have implemented new service processes with a burst of energy...then everything fizzles after that. Like everything else, there has to be just as much (if not more) time spent on the sustaining side of the equation, as on the introduction side.

When developing your next service process (or any process for that matter), consider four key areas that the Baldrige framework addresses (A.D.L.I.). They are:

Approach - Is the process effective, repeatable, and systematic?

Deployment - Is the process used and understood by everyone who's supposed to know about it?

Learning - What is being learned from this process? Is the process itself being evaluated and improved?

Integration - Is the process working "harmoniously" with other processes in the organization? Or is it just a "loner"...not affecting the way work is done elsewhere?

I know, I know...let me give you an example to make it clear. An office building, Company X, decides that it wants to create a world-class arrival experience for its visitors. So it creates a new arrival process, which entails the receptionist getting up from behind his/her desk and

Has the "purpose" of this new process been explained?

giving a big "Welcome". Then after getting the visitor's name, the receptionist escorts the visitor to the nearby elevator, pushes the elevator button, and explains which floor the visitor should get off at. Of course, this all ends with a big "Have a great day/meeting/lunch/first date"...you get the picture.

Now, let's apply the A.D.L.I. framework to test this new process.

Approach - How often will it be done? Will it be done in every shift for every visitor? Are the service standards in place to effectively train the receptionists? Does this new process align with the company's mission...vision...core values...strategic objectives? Has the "purpose" of this new process been explained?

Deploy - Will all the receptionists be trained? Since the receptionists will be the ones executing this new arrival experience, were they involved in developing the process? Do all of the managers for the office building know and understand the process? Do all of the relevant line staff know and understand the process?

Learning - What results will you capture to know that the process works? How often will you check the results? Will the receptionists have access to the results so they can know the progress being made? How often will you schedule a meeting to review the entire process to see how the arrival experience can be continuously improved?

Integration - Will the service scores be used as considerations during the next strategic planning cycle? Will the new arrival standards be used as a consideration when recruiting and selecting new receptionists? Will the new standards be used when training new receptionists? Will the new process be incorporated into new marketing material when trying to solicit new tenants?

As you can see, if those types of questions are asked when you're developing the next big process, it will stand a much better chance of becoming a part of the company's culture.

Activity – Think About Your Service Framework

Answer the following questions for each of your current service processes. Do the exercise first on your own, and then as part of a team discussion.

Approach - Is the process effective, repeatable, and systematic?

If not, what actions or systems are needed to affect change?

Deployment - Is the process used and understood by everyone who's supposed to know about it?

If not, what actions or systems are needed to ensure use and understanding?

Learning - What is being learned from this process? Is the process itself being evaluated and improved?

If not, what educational processes do you need to change, evaluate, and/or improve?

Integration - Is the process working "harmoniously" with other processes in the organization?

If the process is just a "loner"...not affecting the way work is done elsewhere, what can you and/or your team do to create harmony with other processes in the organization?

Recap: Test Your Service Professional Quotient (SPQ)...Again

Now that you have completed "Engaging Service: 22 Ways to Become a Service Superstar," let's re-test your Service Professional Quotient. This time, consider all the lessons learned throughout each chapter and see where your Quotient lands. As always, your continued success is my greatest goal!

~Bryan Williams

1. Using the scale below and the evaluation on the following page, rate your Service Professional Quotient. This is your current level of commitment to deliver a fully engaged customer experience.

1	Strongly disagree
2	Disagree
3	Does not apply
4	Agree
5	Strongly agree

2. Place a check mark in the box under the number that most closely matches your current environment and/or ability to deliver on service.
3. For all questions rated 1 or 2, collaborate with your Supervisor or Mentor to plan actions for improvement.
4. For questions rated "4," identify a plan actions to get to a "5" rating.

Statement	1	2	3	4	5
I am proud of what my company has to offer and it shows with each customer interaction.					
I am proud of what I personally offer as a Service Professional and it shows with each customer interaction.					
My team's culture requires and supports doing whatever it takes to make each of my customers feel valued and appreciated.					
I personally make sure each of my customers feels valued and appreciated.					
I make sure every customer I serve will remember me because of the exceptional service I consistently extend.					
I personalize my service by making sure I connect (eye contact, voice connection, etc.) with the customer and use the customer's preferred name.					

Statement	1	2	3	4	5
My company gives me permission to take personal ownership of customer complaints					
I take personal ownership of customer complaints					
I follow through with complaint resolution until the customer is completely satisfied					
My company and Supervisor empower me to follow through with complaint resolution until the customer is completely satisfied					
I take time to research my customer base… who I will be serving …and learn about their preference					
I am always thinking of ways to not only meet, but *exceed* customer expectations					
My company and Supervisor empower me to offer additional assistance to customers					
I always offer additional assistance to customers					

Action Plan – Improve Your SPQ

How are you doing now? As before, all statements rated a **1, 2,** or **4** are now goals for improvement. Use your Day Planner or the provided table (next page) to:

5. List Goals for improvement (first column)
6. Collaborate on steps needed to improve performance. Think outside the box!
7. Set dates with your Supervisor/Mentor for when you expect to see improvement.
8. Set a date to re-evaluate and make sure you have improved your Service Professional Quotient.

As you work toward improvement, think about ways you can see every experience through the eyes of the customer.

Goal	Action	By...
Follow through when resolving complaints	• Listen (really listen) to the complaint • List (mentally or on paper) what needs to happen for improvement • Confirm the list with the customer… "What I hear you saying is you need to see A, B, and C to help make this a better experience. Is that correct?" • Work the list • Follow up with the customer and with teammates who you've asked to help deliver (e.g., Accounting Supervisor who can make system changes that you are unauthorized to complete) • Continue until the complaint is resolved ***to the customers delight***	10/20/09

Your Personal SPQ Action Plan

Goal	Action	By...

Find more articles relating to service excellence at
www.bwenterprise.net.

Also on the website, you can subscribe to the official
B.Williams Enterprise emailing list. You will receive
announcements, newsletters and other excellent resources.

Shop for your customer service products at
www.engagemenow.com

-We exist to serve others so they may better serve the world®.-

ENTERPRISE ®

CPSIA information can be obtained at www.ICGtesting.com
Printed in the USA
BVOW02s2022230713

326671BV00001B/4/P